TEACHER RECOMMENDED

1ˢᵗ GRADE
COMMON CORE
MATH

DAILY PRACTICE BOOK

ARGOPREP.COM

FREE ONLINE SYSTEM
WITH VIDEO
EXPLANATIONS

ArgoPrep is one of the leading providers of supplemental educational products and services. We offer affordable and effective test prep solutions to educators, parents and students. Learning should be fun and easy! For that reason, most of our workbooks come with detailed video answer explanations taught by one of our fabulous instructors.

Our goal is to make your life easier, so let us know how we can help you by e-mailing us at: info@argoprep.com.

Aknowlegments:
Icons made by Freepik, Creaticca Creative Agency, Pixel perfect , Pixel Buddha, Smashicons, Twitter , Good Ware, Smalllikeart, Nikita Golubev, monkik, DinosoftLabs, Icon Pond from www.flaticon.com

Our Awards

- ArgoPrep is a recipient of the prestigious **Mom's Choice Award**.

- ArgoPrep also received the 2019 **Seal of Approval** from Homeschool.com for our award-winning workbooks.

- ArgoPrep was awarded the 2019 **National Parenting Products Award, Gold Medal Parent's Choice Award** and **the Tillywig Brain Child Award.**

Want an amazing offer from ArgoPrep?

7 DAY ACCESS

to our online premium content at:
www.argoprep.com/k8

Online premium content includes practice quizzes and drills with video explanations and an automatic grading system.

Chat with us live at **www.argoprep.com/k8** for this exclusive offer.

TABLE OF
CONTENTS

HOW TO USE THE BOOK

This workbook is designed to give lots of practice with the math Common Core State Standards (CCSS). By practicing and mastering this entire workbook, your child will become very familiar and comfortable with the state math exam. If you are a teacher using this workbook for your students, you will notice each question is labeled with the specific standard so you can easily assign your students problems in the workbook. This workbook takes the CCSS and divides them up among 20 weeks. By working on these problems on a daily basis, students will be able to (1) find any deficiencies in their understanding and/or practice of math and (2) have small successes each day that will build proficiency and confidence in their abilities.

We strongly recommend watching the videos, as they will reinforce the fundamental concepts. Please note, scrap paper may be necessary while using this workbook so that the student has sufficient space to show their work.

For a detailed overview of the Common Core State Standards for 1st grade, please visit: www.corestandards.org/Math/Content/1/introduction/

How to access video explantions?

Download our app: **ArgoPrep Video Explanations** to access videos on any mobile device or tablet.

You also can access it on our website:

Step 1 - Visit our website at: www.argoprep.com/k8

Step 2 - Click on the Video Explanations button located on the top right corner.

Step 3 - Choose the workbook you have and enjoy video explanations.

OTHER BOOKS BY ARGOPREP

Here are some other test prep workbooks by ArgoPrep you may be interested in. All of our workbooks come equipped with detailed video explanations to make your learning experience a breeze! Visit us at **www.argoprep.com**

COMMON CORE MATH SERIES

 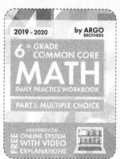  

COMMON CORE ELA SERIES

   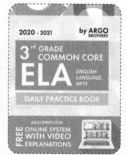 

INTRODUCING MATH!

Introducing Math! by ArgoPrep is an award-winning series created by certified teachers to provide students with high-quality practice problems. Our workbooks include topic overviews with instruction, practice questions, answer explanations along with digital access to video explanations. Practice in confidence - with ArgoPrep!

SCIENCE SERIES

Science Daily Practice Workbook by ArgoPrep is an award-winning series created by certified science teachers to help build mastery of foundational science skills. Our workbooks explore science topics in depth with ArgoPrep s 5 E S to build science mastery.

KIDS SUMMER ACADEMY SERIES

ArgoPrep's **Kids Summer Academy** series helps prevent summer learning loss and gets students ready for their new school year by reinforcing core foundations in math, english and science. Our workbooks also introduce new concepts so students can get a head start and be on top of their game for the new school year!

SUMMER ACTIVITY PLAYGROUND SERIES

Summer Activity Playground is another summer series that is designed to prevent summer learning loss and prepares students for the new school year. Students will be able to practice math, ELA, science, social studies and more! This is a new released series that offers the latest aligned learning standards for each grade.

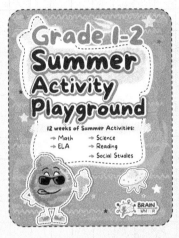
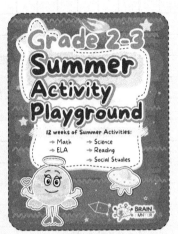

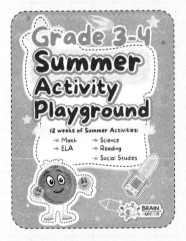
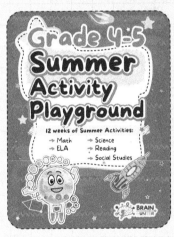

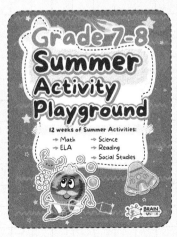

Download our app:
ArgoPrep Video Explanations to access videos on any mobile device or tablet.

Week 1 is all about adding and subtracting within 20 to solve word problems. Let's get started!

You can find detailed video explanations of each problem in the book by visiting:
ArgoPrep.com

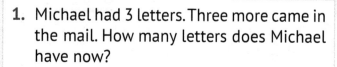

1. Michael had 3 letters. Three more came in the mail. How many letters does Michael have now?

$$3 + 3 = \boxed{}$$

A. 5
B. 6
C. 7
D. 8

1.OA.A.1

2. Jamie has 7 apples. Jamie eats 2 apples. How many apples does Jamie have left?

$$7 - 2 = \boxed{}$$

A. 3
B. 4
C. 5
D. 6

1.OA.A.1

3. There were 15 strawberries on the table. Lisa ate some strawberries. Then there were 7 strawberries. How many strawberries did Lisa eat?

$$15 - \boxed{} = 7$$

A. 5
B. 7
C. 8
D. 10

1.OA.A.1

4. Ms. Smith has 8 chocolates. She ate 2 of them. How many chocolates does she have left?

$$8 - 2 = \boxed{}$$

A. 3
B. 4
C. 5
D. 6

1.OA.A.1

5. There were some books on the table. 6 more books were placed on the table. Now there is a total of 13 books on the table. How many books were on the table before?

$$\boxed{} + 6 = 13$$

A. 5
B. 7
C. 8
D. 9

1.OA.A.1

6. Eight red apples and 2 green apples are in the basket. How many apples are in the basket?

$$8 + 2 = \boxed{}$$

A. 9
B. 10
C. 11
D. 12

1.OA.A.1

TIP of the DAY

Look for keywords that help you understand whether you need to add or subtract for any given problem.

12

1. Lisa has 5 more peaches than Tony. Tony has 11 peaches. How many peaches does Lisa have?

$$11 + 5 = \boxed{}$$

A. 6
B. 16
C. 17
D. 19

1.OA.A.1

4. I had 11 candies. My brother ate some and I was left with 6 candies. How many candies did my brother eat?

$$11 - \boxed{} = 6$$

A. 5
B. 7
C. 9
D. 11

1.OA.A.1

2. Simon has 3 fewer oranges than Jessica. Jessica has 17 oranges. How many oranges does Simon have?

$$17 - 3 = \boxed{}$$

_____ 1.OA.A.1

5. There are 6 cats and 14 dogs. How many animals are there together?

$$6 + 14 = \boxed{}$$

_____ 1.OA.A.1

3. Luis had 10 books. He gave 6 books to his sister. How many books does Luis have now?

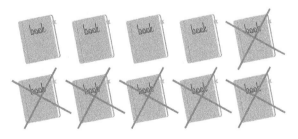

A. 2   C. 5
B. 4   D. 8

1.OA.A.1

6. How many flowers do you see?

_____ 1.OA.A.1

TIP
of the
DAY

If you are stuck with a particular question, try to draw a diagram to help you visualize the answer.

1. There were 9 baseballs. Three baseballs got lost. How many baseballs are there remaining?

A. 10   D. 6
B. 8
C. 7   1.OA.A.1

2. There are 20 stamps. Lisa uses 8 stamps. How many stamps are left?

20 - 8 = ☐

There are _____ stamps left.   1.OA.A.1

3. Ria has 7 carrots. Liza has 19 carrots. How many more carrots does Liza have than Ria?

19 - 7 = ☐

A. 10
B. 12
C. 13
D. 15   1.OA.A.1

4. There are 8 roses in a flower vase. Four more roses are added to the flower vase. How many roses are in the flower vase?

8 + 4 = ☐

A. 10
B. 12
C. 14
D. 15   1.OA.A.1

5. There are 7 birds. Three flew away. How many birds remain?

_____ birds remain.   1.OA.A.1

6. How many bananas do you see?

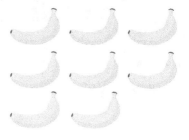

_____   1.OA.A.1

TIP
of the
DAY

Do you have trouble counting numbers? Using marbles or other small objects to help you count is a great way to learn.

1. There are 4 blue cars and 3 red cars. How many total cars are there?

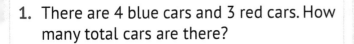

There are _____ total cars.

1.OA.A.1

2. Bob has 2 fewer siblings than Ron. Ron has 5 siblings. How many siblings does Bob have?

$$5 - 2 = \boxed{}$$

A. 3
B. 4
C. 5
D. 6

1.OA.A.1

3. There were 12 stickers in a book. Mike used 5 stickers from the book. How many stickers remain?

$$12 - 5 = \boxed{}$$

_____ stickers remain.

1.OA.A.1

4. The red rug is 19 inches long in length. The yellow rug is 3 inches shorter than the red rug. How many inches long is the yellow rug in length?

$$19 - 3 = \boxed{}$$

The yellow rug is _____ inches in length.

1.OA.A.1

5. There are 3 birds. Two more birds fly in. How many birds are there in total?

A. 3   D. 6
B. 4
C. 5

1.OA.A.1

6. There were 18 apples in a basket. Sally eats 5 apples. Mike eats 3 apples. How many apples remain in the basket?

$$18 - 5 = \boxed{}$$
$$\boxed{} - 3 = \boxed{}$$

There are _____ apples remaining in the basket.

1.OA.A.1

TIP of the DAY

This week we are practicing our addition and subtraction skills for numbers 1 through 20. Can you add or subtract mentally without using your fingers? Try it!

1. How many guitars are there in the picture shown below?

There are _____ guitars shown in the picture.

1.OA.A.1

2. There are 17 cats in the animal shelter. The Brady family adopted 3 cats from the animal shelter. How many cats remain in the animal shelter?

$$17 - 3 = \boxed{}$$

A. 11
B. 14
C. 15
D. 16

1.OA.A.1

3. Lisa had 12 pencils in her pencil case. Two of the pencils broke and had to be thrown away. How many pencils remain in the pencil case?

$$12 - 2 = \boxed{}$$

A. 2
B. 8
C. 10
D. 12

1.OA.A.1

4. There are 14 cars in a parking lot. The cars are either black or red. There are 8 red cards in the parking lot. How many black cars are there?

There are _____ black cars in the parking lot.

1.OA.A.1

5. Fill in the missing number.

$$7 + \boxed{} = 19$$

A. 7
B. 10
C. 12
D. 13

1.OA.A.1

DAY 6
Challenge qvestion

There were 19 apples in a basket. Holly eats 2 apples. Mike eats 4 apples. Jessica eats 3 apples. How many apples remain in the basket?

There are _____ apples remaining in the basket.

1.OA.A.1

16

WEEK 2

VIDEO EXPLANATIONS

ARGOPREP.COM

This week we are going to solve word problems that involve three whole numbers and we are going to practice our addition skills.

You can find detailed video explanations of each problem in the book by visiting:
ArgoPrep.com

1. There are 5 blue cars, 2 red cars, and 3 green cars in a parking lot. How many cars are in the parking lot?

There are _____ cars in the parking lot

1.OA.A.2

2. There are 3 red apples, 7 yellow apples, and 4 green apples. How many apples are there in total?

$$3 + 7 + 4 = \square$$

A. 10
B. 13
C. 14
D. 17

1.OA.A.2

3. Solve for the blank box.

$$8 + \square + 3 = 13$$

A. 1
B. 2
C. 3
D. 5

1.OA.A.2

4. Solve for the blank box.

$$\square + 3 + 9 = 20$$

A. 4
B. 6
C. 7
D. 8

1.OA.A.2

5. There are four red balloons, six green balloons, and nine white balloons in the party. How many total balloons are in the party?

There is a total of _____ balloons in the party.

1.OA.A.2

6. Which number completes the number sentence?

$$7 + 2 + \square = 16$$

A. 5
B. 7
C. 8
D. 10

1.OA.A.2

TIP of the DAY

The words "add," "altogether," and "both" are keywords that tell us we need to use addition to solve the problem.

WEEK 2 : DAY 2

1. There are 4 red roses, 5 tulips and 7 carnations in the flower vase. How many total flowers are there in the vase?

$$4 + 5 + 7 = \boxed{}$$

A. 9
B. 15
C. 16
D. 17

1.OA.A.2

2. John has 6 cookies. Tom has 6 cookies. Bill has 4 cookies. How many cookies do they have in total?

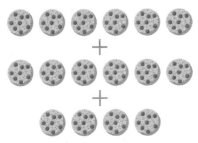

A. 12   C. 16
B. 14   D. 18

1.OA.A.2

3. Solve for the blank box.

$$9 + \boxed{} + 2 = 20$$

A. 7   C. 11
B. 9   D. 16

1.OA.A.2

4. There are 11 oranges, 3 apples, and 4 peaches in a shopping cart. How many fruits in total are there in the shopping cart?

$$11 + 3 + 4 = \boxed{}$$

A. 13
B. 15
C. 18
D. 19

1.OA.A.2

5. Which number completes the number sentence?

$$4 + 11 + \boxed{} = 15$$

A. 0
B. 1
C. 3
D. 6

1.OA.A.2

6. Julia has seven baseball cards. Matt gives her three additional baseball cards. Jacob gives Julia another four baseball cards. How many baseball cards does Julia have in total?

A. 7
B. 10
C. 13
D. 14

1.OA.A.2

TIP of the DAY

The words "increased by," "gain," "raise," and "more" are keywords that tell us we need to use addition to solve the problem.

1. How many toy blocks do you see in total?

   A. 7
   B. 10
   C. 11
   D. 13

   1.OA.A.2

2. Which number completes the number sentence?

$$6 + 1 + \boxed{} = 13$$

   A. 4
   B. 5
   C. 6
   D. 7

   1.OA.A.2

3. There are 18 birds. Three fly away. How many birds remain?

   _____ birds remain.

   1.OA.A.2

4. Solve for the blank box.

$$9 + \boxed{} + 1 = 20$$

   A. 7
   B. 8
   C. 9
   D. 10

   1.OA.A.2

5. Jim places 8 green marbles in a bag. Tony places 4 blue marbles in the same bag. Julie places 8 yellow marbles in the same bag. How many marbles are now in the bag?

   A. 10
   B. 12
   C. 18
   D. 20

   1.OA.A.2

6. Paul buys 2 green T-shirts, 7 yellow T-shirts and 3 gray T-shirts. How many T-shirts did Paul buy in total?

   Paul bought _____ T-shirts in total.

   1.OA.A.2

TIP of the DAY

The words "more than," "sum," and "together" are keywords that tell us we need to use addition to solve the problem.

1. Tim drew 10 triangles. He then erased 2 triangles. How many triangles remain?

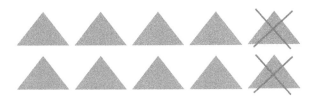

A. 2
B. 8
C. 10
D. 12

1.OA.A.2

2. There are 6 black motorcycles, 7 red motorcycles and 3 white motorcycles. How many total motorcycles are there?

$$6 + 7 + 3 = \boxed{}$$

_____

1.OA.A.2

3. How many keys do you see?

There are _____ keys

1.OA.A.2

4. Which number completes the number sentence?

$$\boxed{} + 16 + 3 = 20$$

A. 0
B. 1
C. 2
D. 3

1.OA.A.2

5. Solve for the blank box.

$$6 + \boxed{} + 3 = 11$$

A. 2
B. 4
C. 5
D. 7

1.OA.A.2

6. Chris has 5 blue fish, 3 orange fish, and 2 green fish in his fish tank. How many fish does he have in all?

A. 7
B. 8
C. 10
D. 12

1.OA.A.2

TIP
of the DAY

The words "went away," "take away," and "difference" are keywords that tell us we need to use subtraction to solve the problem.

WEEK 2 : DAY 5

1. Marco is picking flowers for his grandma. He picks 3 daisies, 7 sunflowers, and 2 tulips. How many flowers does he pick in all?

   A. 10
   B. 11
   C. 12
   D. 13

   1.OA.A.2

2. John lives on a farm. His family has 4 goats, 9 sheep, and 3 cows. How many animals do they have in all?

   A. 13
   B. 14
   C. 15
   D. 16

   1.OA.A.2

3. Jace is counting his candy from trick-or-treating. He counts 6 cherry lollipops, 2 orange lollipops, and 9 grape lollipops. How many lollipops does he have in all?

   A. 14
   B. 17
   C. 19
   D. 20

   1.OA.A.2

4. The big cat exhibit at the zoo has 4 tigers, 2 lions, and 10 leopards. How many big cats are there in all?

   A. 15
   B. 16
   C. 18
   D. 19

   1.OA.A.2

5. Which number completes the number sentence?

   $$11 + 1 + \boxed{} = 17$$

   A. 3
   B. 5
   C. 8
   D. 12

   1.OA.A.2

6. Solve the following.

   $$14 + 3 + 2 = \boxed{}$$

   A. 16
   B. 17
   C. 19
   D. 20

   1.OA.A.2

DAY 6
Challenge qvestion

All of the first grade rooms at Douglass School have class pets. Mr. Watson's class has 7 hamsters. Ms. Wong's class has 4 fish. Ms. Taylor's class has 6 turtles. How many class pets are there in all?

There are _____ class pets in total.

1.OA.A.2

22

Week 3 is all about learning the properties of operations. We will learn about the commutative property and associative property of addition.

You can find detailed video explanations of each problem in the book by visiting:
ArgoPrep.com

1. Fill in the blank:

$$8 + 6 = 8 + 2 + \square$$

A. 2
B. 3
C. 4
D. 6

1.OA.B.3

2. ▲ is a mystery number. 5 + ▲ = 14. What is ▲ + 5 ?

A. 3
B. 5
C. 11
D. 14

1.OA.B.3

3. Fill in the blank:

$$9 + 3 = 9 + \square + 1$$

A. 1
B. 2
C. 3
D. 4

1.OA.B.3

4. 36 + 54 = 90. What is 54 + 36?

_____

1.OA.B.3

5. Which of the following is the same as

$$8 + 1 = 9?$$

A. 1 + 7 = 8
B. 1 + 9 = 8
C. 8 + 0 = 8
D. 1 + 8 = 9

1.OA.B.3

6. Which model has the same value as 3 + 1?

A. ⬤⬤⬤ + ⬤⬤

B. ◤◤◤◤◤ + ◤◤◤

C. ◯ + ◯◯◯

D. ◯◯◯ + ◯◯◯

1.OA.B.3

TIP
of the
DAY

A fun way to learn how to count to 100 is having a jar full of pennies! Count 100 pennies and then divide the pennies into groups of 10.

24

1. △ is a mystery number. $8 + △ = 12$. What is $△ + 8$?

A. 5
B. 7
C. 8
D. 12

1.OA.B.3

2. Which of the following is the same as

$$4 + 14 = 18?$$

A. $10 + 4 = 14$
B. $14 + 18 = 32$
C. $14 + 4 = 18$
D. $18 + 0 = 18$

1.OA.B.3

3. $15 + 12 = 27$. What is $12 + 15$?

_____

1.OA.B.3

4. Fill in the blank:

$$12 + 8 = 12 + 4 + \boxed{}$$

A. 0
B. 4
C. 8
D. 12

1.OA.B.3

5. Fill in the blank:

$$19 + 11 = 19 + \boxed{} + 10$$

A. 1
B. 5
C. 11
D. 19

1.OA.B.3

6. ▦ is a mystery number. $▦ + 9 = 100$. What is $9 + ▦$?

A. 0
B. 8
C. 9
D. 100

1.OA.B.3

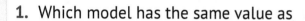

1. Which model has the same value as

1 + 4?

A.

B.

C.

D.

1.OA.B.3

2. ■ is a mystery number. ■ + 11 = 27. What is 11 + ■ ?

A. 11
B. 16
C. 27
D. 38

1.OA.B.3

3. 12 + 11 = 23. What is 11 + 12?

_____

1.OA.B.3

4. Which of the following is the same as 9 + 10 = 19?

A. 1 + 9 = 10
B. 9 + 11 = 20
C. 5 + 10 = 15
D. 10 + 9 = 19

1.OA.B.3

5. Fill in the blank:

9 + 14 = 9 + 1 + ☐

A. 1
B. 9
C. 13
D. 14

1.OA.B.3

6. Fill in the blank:

20 + 7 = 20 + ☐ + 2

A. 0
B. 3
C. 5
D. 20

1.OA.B.3

TIP of the DAY

Never leave a question blank on the exam. If you do not know the answer, make an educated guess.

26

1. Which of the following is the same as 83 + 10 = 93?

   A. 50 + 20 = 70
   B. 93 - 20 = 73
   C. 10 + 83 = 93
   D. 83 + 93 = 176

1.OA.B.3

4. 12 + 7 + 10 = 29. What is 10 + 7 + 12?

   A. 7
   B. 19
   C. 12
   D. 29

1.OA.B.3

2. is a mystery number. 40 + = 43. What is + 40?

   A. 3
   B. 40
   C. 43
   D. 46

1.OA.B.3

5. Fill in the blank:

$$16 + 13 = 16 + \boxed{} + 0$$

   A. 0
   B. 5
   C. 13
   D. 16

1.OA.B.3

3. 72 + 13 = 85. What is 13 + 72?

_____

1.OA.B.3

6. Fill in the blank:

$$29 + 11 = 29 + 3 + \boxed{}$$

   A. 3
   B. 8
   C. 11
   D. 29

1.OA.B.3

TIP of the DAY

The plug and check method is a great way to solve a Multiple Choice question when you are unsure of the answer.

WEEK 3 : DAY 5

ASSESSMENT

1. ▲ is a mystery number. 24 + ▲ = 98. What is ▲ + 24 ?

  A. 24
  B. 74
  C. 98
  D. 122

1.OA.B.3

2. Fill in the blank:

$$12 + 20 = 20 + 7 + \square$$

  A. 5
  B. 7
  C. 12
  D. 20

1.OA.B.3

3. Which of the following is the same as

$$23 + 35 = 58?$$

  A. 35 + 23 = 58
  B. 23 + 45 = 68
  C. 13 + 30 = 43
  D. 20 + 5 = 25

1.OA.B.3

4. 14 + 19 = 33. What is 19 + 14?

_____

1.OA.B.3

5. ■ is a mystery number. ■ + 53 = 99. What is 53 + ■ ?

_____

1.OA.B.3

6. 11 + 17 + 20 = 48. What is 20 + 17 + 11?

  A. 11
  B. 17
  C. 20
  D. 48

1.OA.B.3

DAY 6

Challenge qvestion

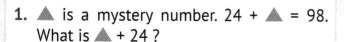 is a mystery number. 23 + ● = 72. What is ● + 23?

_____

1.OA.B.3

WEEK 4

VIDEO EXPLANATIONS ▶ ARGOPREP.COM

Subtraction is related to addition. In Week 4 we will learn about subtraction as an unknown-addend problem.

You can find detailed video explanations of each problem in the book by visiting:
ArgoPrep.com

1. Which number can complete BOTH number sentences?

$5 +$ ☐ $= 11$ $11 - 5 =$ ☐

A. 3
B. 5
C. 6
D. 11

1.OA.B.4

2. Tamia needs 10 apples to make a pie. She already has 5 apples. Which number sentence shows how many more apples Tamia needs?

A. $10 - 5 =$ ☐

B. $10 + 5 =$ ☐

C. ☐ $- 10 = 5$

D. $10 +$ ☐ $= 5$

1.OA.B.4

3. Which number can complete BOTH number sentences?

☐ $+ 8 = 10$ $10 - 8 =$ ☐

Answer: _____

1.OA.B.4

4. You can use the number sentence to make all of the following new number sentences, **EXCEPT...**

A. $5 + 15 = 20$
B. $15 + 5 = 20$
C. $15 - 5 = 10$
D. $15 - 10 = 10$

1.OA.B.4

5. ▶ is a mystery number. ▶ $+ 7 = 12$. What is $12 -$ ▶ ?

A. 3
B. 5
C. 7
D. 12

1.OA.B.4

6. ▶ is a mystery number. ▶ $+ 24 = 100$. What is $100 -$ ▶ ?

_____

1.OA.B.4

TIP
of the
DAY

Try reading the math problems out loud so you can hear the problem and think about what the question is asking you.

1. There are 23 students in a classroom. 14 of them are girls. How many boys are there?

   A. 5
   B. 9
   C. 14
   D. 37

   1.OA.B.4

2. ■ is a mystery number. ■ + 42 = 97. What is 97 - ■ ?

   _____

   1.OA.B.4

3. You can use the number sentence to make all of the following new number sentences, **EXCEPT...**

   A. 5 + 7 = 12
   B. 12 - 7 = 5
   C. 7 + 3 = 12
   D. 7 - 3 = 4

   1.OA.B.4

4. Martin is buying bagels. He needs to buy 22 bagels. He already has 9 bagels in his bag. Which number sentence shows how many more bagels Martin needs to buy?

   A. $22 + 9 = \square$

   B. $22 + \square = 9$

   C. $9 + \square = 22$

   D. $9 - \square = 22$

   1.OA.B.4

5. Which number can complete BOTH number sentences?

   $$7 + \square = 20 \qquad 20 - 7 = \square$$

   A. 3
   B. 7
   C. 13
   D. 27

   1.OA.B.4

6. Which number can complete BOTH number sentences?

   $$\square + 12 = 24 \qquad 24 - 12 = \square$$

   Answer: _____

   1.OA.B.4

TIP of the DAY

Learning math can be fun! Try playing the "I am thinking of a number..." game!
I am thinking of a number that equals 5 when it is added to 3. What is the number?

31

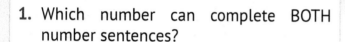

1. Which number can complete BOTH number sentences?

☐ + 10 = 30   30 - 10 = ☐

_____

1.OA.B.4

4. ▶ is a mystery number. ▶ + 66 = 89. What is 89 - ▶ ?

_____

1.OA.B.4

2. You can use the number sentence to make all of the following new number sentences, **EXCEPT**...

A. 17 + 3 = 20
B. 17 - 3 = 15
C. 20 + 3 = 23
D. 20 - 3 = 17

1.OA.B.4

5. Which number can complete BOTH number sentences?

7 + ☐ = 20   20 - 7 = ☐

A. 5
B. 7
C. 13
D. 15

1.OA.B.4

3. There are 30 students in Ms. Smith's class. 12 of the students are boys. How many girls are there?

There are _____ girls in Ms. Smith's class.

1.OA.B.4

6. ■ is a mystery number. ■ + 50 = 100. What is 100 - ■ ?

A. 25
B. 50
C. 75
D. 100

1.OA.B.4

TIP of the DAY

Subtraction is related to addition. For example, 3 + 2 = 5, 5 – 2 = 3 and 5 – 3 = 2. The same three numbers are in all of the number sentences. The answer to a subtraction problem is called the difference.

1. Ella ate 5 chocolates. Bryson also ate some chocolates. They ate 15 chocolates in all. Which number sentence will NOT help you find the number of chocolates that Bryson ate?

   A. $15 - 5 = \Box$

   B. $5 + 15 = \Box$

   C. $5 + \Box = 15$

   D. $\Box + 5 = 15$

   1.OA.B.4

2. Susan is buying oranges. She needs to buy 17 oranges. Susan already has 9 oranges in her basket. Which number sentence shows how many more oranges Susan needs to place in her basket?

   A. $17 + 9 = \Box$

   B. $9 + 17 = \Box$

   C. $17 - 5 = \Box$

   D. $17 - 9 = \Box$

   1.OA.B.4

3. Which number can complete BOTH number sentences?

   $11 + \Box = 13$ $13 - 11 = \Box$

   A. 0

   B. 1

   C. 2

   D. 4

   1.OA.B.4

4. You can use the number sentence   to make all of the following new number sentences, EXCEPT...

   A. $11 + 9 = 20$

   B. $20 - 9 = 11$

   C. $15 + 3 = 17$

   D. $15 - 3 = 12$

   1.OA.B.4

5. ▶ is a mystery number. ▶ + 40 = 80. What is 80 - ▶ ?

   A. 20

   B. 40

   C. 80

   D. 100

   1.OA.B.4

TIP
of the
DAY

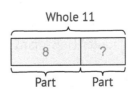

Whole 11

8	?
Part	Part

When finding the missing number in a subtraction problem, think of using a bar model to find the answer.

Subtract to find the part 11 - 8 = 3

1. John ate 3 apples. Lisa also ate some apples. They ate 5 apples in all. Which number sentence will help you find the number of apples that Lisa ate?

A. $3 + 5 = \square$

B. $5 + \square = 3$

C. $3 + \square = 5$

D. $8 + 3 = \square$

1.OA.B.4

2. ▇ is a mystery number. ▇ $+ 55 = 88$. What is $88 - $ ▇ ?

A. 33
B. 55
C. 88
D. 143

1.OA.B.4

3. Which number can complete BOTH number sentences?

$\square + 20 = 35$ $35 - 20 = \square$

A. 10
B. 15
C. 20
D. 25

1.OA.B.4

4. You can use the number sentence to make all of the following new number sentences, **EXCEPT...**

A. $11 + 4 = 15$
B. $11 - 4 = 7$
C. $19 - 3 = 17$
D. $19 + 3 = 22$

1.OA.B.4

5. Which number can complete BOTH number sentences?

$19 + \square = 24$ $24 - 19 = \square$

_____

1.OA.B.4

6. ▶ is a mystery number. ▶ $+ 71 = 100$. What is $100 - $ ▶ ?

_____

1.OA.B.4

DAY 6
Challenge qvestion

There are 50 people in the park. 32 of them are kids. The rest are adults. How many adults are in the park?

There are _____ adults in the park

1.OA.B.4

WEEK 5

ARGOPREP.COM

VIDEO
EXPLANATIONS ▶

Get ready to count in Week 5. We will add and subtract numbers within 20.

You can find detailed video explanations of each problem in the book by visiting:
ArgoPrep.com

1. Which picture shows 9 + 3?

A.

B.

C.

D.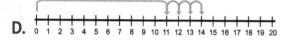

1.OA.C.5

2. Jake has 10 gumballs. He counts 3 gumballs and gives them to his friends. Which number sentence shows how many gumballs Jake has left?

A. 10 + 3 = 13
B. 10 - 3 = 7
C. 3 - 10 = 13
D. 3 + 7 = 10

1.OA.C.5

3. Maggie starts at the number 16. She counts on 5 more. What number does Maggie end on?

_____

1.OA.C.5

4. Xavier starts at the number 15. He counts back 3. What number does Xavier end on?

_____

1.OA.C.5

5. Alex is adding 8 + 3. He should start at the number ____ and count on 3.

A. 0
B. 3
C. 5
D. 8

1.OA.C.5

6. James is subtracting 11 – 8. He should start at the number 11 and count back

_____

A. 3
B. 5
C. 8
D. 11

1.OA.C.5

TIP *of the* **DAY**

When doing different kinds of problems, take time to remember the same kinds of problems that you did before.

1. Katie starts at the number 21. She counts back 7. What number does Katie end on?

   A. 7
   B. 10
   C. 14
   D. 18

   1.OA.C.5

4. Luis has 12 oranges. He gives 4 of the oranges to his friends. Which number sentence shows how many oranges Luis has left?_____

   A. 12 + 4 = 16
   B. 16 - 4 = 12
   C. 12 - 16 = 4
   D. 12 - 4 = 8

   1.OA.C.5

2. Liza is adding 12 + 9. She should start at the number ____ and count on 9.

   A. 3
   B. 9
   C. 12
   D. 21

   1.OA.C.5

5. Ron starts at the number 13. He counts on 9 more. What number does Ron end on?

   _____

   1.OA.C.5

3. Jeremy is subtracting 23 – 2. He should start at the number 23 and count back _____

   A. 2
   B. 21
   C. 23
   D. 25

   1.OA.C.5

6. Ashley starts at the number 20. She counts on 5 more. She then counts back 3. What number does Ashley end on?

   A. 15
   B. 22
   C. 25
   D. 28

   1.OA.C.5

TIP of the DAY

The answer to an addition problem is called the "sum".
For example, the sum of 3 + 2 is 5.
3 + 2 = 5

WEEK 5 : DAY 3

1. Lindsey starts at the number 30. She counts on 7 more. She then counts back 4. What number does Lindsey end on?

A. 7
B. 33
C. 37
D. 41

1.OA.C.5

2. Michael starts at the number 19. He counts on 7 more. What number does Michael end on?

_____

1.OA.C.5

3. Cory starts at the number 15. He counts back 13. What number does Corey end on?

_____

1.OA.C.5

4. Which picture shows 8 + 4 ?

A.

B.

C.

D.

1.OA.C.5

5. Kate has 14 bananas. She eats 3 of the bananas. Which number sentence shows how many bananas Kate has left?

A. 14 - 3 = 11
B. 14 + 3 = 17
C. 17 + 3 = 20
D. 17 + 14 = 31

1.OA.C.5

6. Mira has 9 marbles. She counts 3 marbles, and gives them to her friends. How many marbles does Mira have left?

_____

1.OA.C.5

TIP of the DAY

When adding two numbers, you can change the order and still get the same answer. For example, 4 + 1 = 1 + 4.

1. Which picture shows 13 - 5 ?

A.

B.

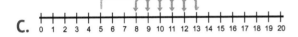
C.

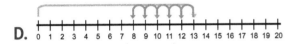
D.

1.OA.C.5

4. There are 10 movie tickets left for sale. The Smith family purchases 6 movie tickets. Which statement below shows how many movie tickets are left for sale?

A. 5 + 6 = 11
B. 10 + 6 = 16
C. 10 - 6 = 4
D. 6 + 4 = 10

1.OA.C.5

2. If I start at the number 29 and count back 4, what number do I end up on?

_____

1.OA.C.5

5. Jerry starts at the number 10. He counts back 9. He then counts forward 15. What number does Jerry end on?

_____

1.OA.C.5

3. If I start at the number 37 and count on 9, what number do I end up on?

_____

1.OA.C.5

6. Julie has 15 apples. She gives 3 of the apples to her friends. Write a number sentence that will help you solve how many apples Julie has remaining.

_____

1.OA.C.5

TIP of the DAY

When adding two numbers, count from the larger number up to 10, then add on the rest of the smaller number. For some, it is easier to add from 10. For example, 9 + 3 = 10 + 2 = 12.

1. Sam and Becca have a total of 15 peaches. Becca has 10 peaches. Write a number sentence that will help you solve how many peaches Sam has.

_____

1.OA.C.5

2. If I start at the number 20 and count back 8, what number do I end up on?

_____

1.OA.C.5

3. Liza starts at the number 24. She counts on 8 more. She then counts back 8. What number does Liza end on?

A. 8
B. 16
C. 24
D. 32

1.OA.C.5

4. Ms. Dale has 20 pencils. She counts 7 pencils and gives them to her students. How many pencils does Ms. Dale have left?

A. 7
B. 12
C. 13
D. 27

1.OA.C.5

5. Michelle has 8 slices of pizza. She gives 6 slices away to her friends. Which number sentence shows how many slices Michelle has left over for herself.

A. 6 + 8 = 14
B. 14 - 6 = 8
C. 14 - 8 = 6
D. 8 - 6 = 2

1.OA.C.5

6. If I start at the number 15 and count forward 7, what number do I end on?

_____

1.OA.C.5

DAY 6
Challenge qvestion

Katy starts at the number 35. She counts on 5 more. She then counts back 6. She then counts back another 6. What number does Katy end on?

_____

1.OA.C.5

40

WEEK 6

VIDEO EXPLANATIONS ▶ ARGOPREP.COM

In Week 6 we will learn the SECRETS of how to add and subtract numbers more efficiently. We will create equivalent but easier numbers to work with to help us solve any addition or subtraction problem.

You can find detailed video explanations of each problem in the book by visiting:
ArgoPrep.com

1. 8 + 9 = 8 + 8 + 1 =

- **A.** 16
- **B.** 17
- **C.** 18
- **D.** 19

1.OA.C.6

4. What is 11 + 8 ?

_____

1.OA.C.6

2. 14 - 7 = 14 - 4 - 3 =

- **A.** 5
- **B.** 7
- **C.** 8
- **D.** 9

1.OA.C.6

5. What is 19 - 14 =

_____

1.OA.C.6

3. 8 + 3 = ?

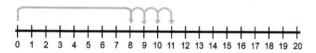

0 1 2 3 4 5 6 7 8 9 10 11 12 13 14 15 16 17 18 19 20

- **A.** 6
- **B.** 8
- **C.** 10
- **D.** 11

1.OA.C.6

6. Mike sees 8 bugs. Kim sees 6 bugs. How many bugs did they see together?

_____ bugs

1.OA.C.6

TIP of the DAY

When regrouping in addition, make sure to remember that 10 ones make a new «ten».

1. Michelle has 4 blue socks and 2 black socks. How many socks does Michelle have in all?

_____ socks

1.OA.C.6

2. 9 + 3 = 9 + 1+ 2

- **A.** 10
- **B.** 11
- **C.** 12
- **D.** 13

1.OA.C.6

3. What is 15 + 3 = ?

_____

1.OA.C.6

4. What is 20 - 12 = ?

_____

1.OA.C.6

5. Jack has 3 cats and 1 dog. Lucy has 4 dogs and 2 cats. How many animals in all do Jack and Lucy have together?

Jack and Lucy have _____ animals.

1.OA.C.6

6. Samantha is making pie. She has 2 green apples, 3 yellow apples, and 3 red apples. How many apples does Samantha have for the pie?

Samantha has _____ apples for her pie

1.OA.C.6

TIP of the DAY

When regrouping in subtraction, make sure to go to the place value to the left to regroup. For example, if you need more tens to subtract, regroup by going to the hundreds place value.

WEEK 6 : DAY 3

1. 13 + 7 = 13 + 2 + 5 =

A. 17
B. 18
C. 19
D. 20

1.OA.C.6

4. What is 13 - 7 = ?

_____

1.OA.C.6

2. 15 - 8 = 15 - 5 - 3 =

A. 3
B. 6
C. 7
D. 10

1.OA.C.6

5. Cindy has 6 marbles. Lia has 3 more marbles than Cindy. How many marbles does Lia have?

Lia has _____ marbles.

1.OA.C.6

3. What is 14 + 6 = ?

_____

1.OA.C.6

6. A certain store had 20 bikes for sale. Three of the bikes were sold. How many bikes remain?

_____ bikes remain.

1.OA.C.6

TIP of the DAY

You can switch the numbers of an addition sentence around to make a subtraction sentence. For example, if 14 + 16 = 30, then make a subtraction sentence that says 30 - 16 = 14, or 30 - 14 = 16. Addition and subtraction are called inverse operations.

44

1. What is 15 - 3 = ?

_____

1.OA.C.6

4. 18 - 11 = 18 - 8 - 3 =

    A. 5
    B. 7
    C. 9
    D. 11

1.OA.C.6

2. Harry has 12 balloons. 5 are blue and the rest are yellow. How many balloons are yellow?

_____ balloons are yellow.

1.OA.C.6

5. 7 + 9 = 7 + 3 + 6 =

    A. 10
    B. 14
    C. 16
    D. 20

1.OA.C.6

3. What is 3 + 9 = ?

    A. 11
    B. 12
    C. 13
    D. 14

1.OA.C.6

6. There are 7 frogs in a pond and 4 frogs on a log. How many frogs are there in all?

    A. 9
    B. 10
    C. 11
    D. 12

1.OA.C.6

TIP of the DAY

8 + 3 = 11
Make this into a subtraction sentence!

WEEK 6 : DAY 5

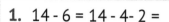

1. 14 - 6 = 14 - 4- 2 =

A. 8
B. 10
C. 12
D. 14

4. Lisa made 14 muffins. She gave away 4 of the muffins to her family. How many muffins does Lisa have remaining?

Lisa has _____ muffins remaining.

1.OA.C.6

2. 12 + 5 = 12 + 3 + 2=

A. 15
B. 17
C. 18
D. 20

1.OA.C.6

5. 11 + 7 = ?

A. 14
B. 16
C. 17
D. 18

1.OA.C.6

3. Ms. Gron plants 8 seeds in her garden. Ms. Ria plants 11 seeds in her garden. How many seeds in total were planted in both gardens?

_____ seeds were planted in both gardens.

1.OA.C.6

6. 13 - 4 = ?

A. 11
B. 10
C. 9
D. 8

1.OA.C.6

DAY 6
Challenge qvestion

Harry ate 2 slices of pizza. His brother ate more than he did. In all, they ate 5 slices of pizza. How many slices did Harry's brother eat?

Harry's brother ate _____ slices of pizza

1.OA.C.6

46

WEEK 7

VIDEO EXPLANATIONS ▶ ARGOPREP.COM

Week 7 is all about understanding the meaning of the equal sign.

You can find detailed video explanations of each problem in the book by visiting:
ArgoPrep.com

WEEK 7 : DAY 1

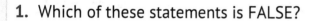

1. Which of these statements is FALSE?

   A. $0 + 3 = 3$
   B. $4 + 2 = 6$
   C. $9 - 7 = 2$
   D. $5 - 3 = 3$

1.OA.D.7

4. Which of these statements is TRUE?

   A. $14 - 7 = 6$
   B. $8 + 3 = 12$
   C. $4 + 3 = 6$
   D. $5 + 6 = 11$

1.OA.D.7

2. Which of these statements is FALSE?

   A. $3 - 1 = 2$
   B. $7 - 3 = 5$
   C. $6 + 3 = 9$
   D. $10 + 4 = 14$

1.OA.D.7

5. Zang and Colby have an equal number of brothers. Zang has 4 brothers. How many brothers does Colby have?

Colby has _____ brothers

1.OA.D.7

3. Which of these statements is TRUE?

   A. $10 - 3 = 8$
   B. $5 - 2 = 4$
   C. $9 - 4 = 5$
   D. $7 + 3 = 11$

1.OA.D.7

6. There are green and red apples in a basket. The number of green apples equals the number of red apples. There are 14 green apples. How many red apples are there?

There are _____ red apples in the basket.

1.OA.D.7

TIP of the DAY

Always make sure to reread word problems and underline the relevant information.

1. Which of these statements is TRUE?

A. 4 + 6 = 9
B. 7 + 2 = 8
C. 1 + 8 = 9
D. 9 - 4 = 2

1.OA.D.7

4. 10 =

 could ONLY be...

A. 5 + 4
B. 10 - 1
C. 5 + 5
D. 7 + 4

1.OA.D.7

2. Which of these statements is FALSE?

A. 9 + 3 = 12
B. 7 - 2 = 4
C. 8 + 3 = 11
D. 11 - 5 = 6

1.OA.D.7

5. Patsy and Joe have the same number of toy trucks. Patsy has 8 trucks. How many trucks does Joe have?

Joe has _____ trucks.

1.OA.D.7

3. Which symbol shows that two amounts are the SAME?

A. +
B. -
C. =
D. >

1.OA.D.7

6. Which of these statements is FALSE?

A. 4 + 2 = 6
B. 11 + 9 = 20
C. 3 - 1 = 2
D. 19 - 7 = 13

1.OA.D.7

TIP *of the* **DAY**

Watch out for keywords such as TRUE or FALSE.

49

WEEK 7 : DAY 3

1. Which of these statements is TRUE?

    A. 5 + 6 = 10
    B. 7 + 2 = 9
    C. 8 - 2 = 4
    D. 9 + 9 = 16

1.OA.D.7

4. 15 = ◆

    ◆ could ONLY be

    A. 3 + 3
    B. 7 - 2
    C. 10 + 5
    D. 9 - 2

1.OA.D.7

2. Which of these statements is FALSE?

    A. 9 + 10 = 19
    B. 20 - 8 = 13
    C. 15 + 4 = 19
    D. 19 - 2 = 17

1.OA.D.7

5. Jessica and Brie have an equal number of cats. Jessica has 3 cats. How many cats does Brie have?

    Brie has _____ cats.

1.OA.D.7

3. Which of these statements is TRUE?

    A. 11 + 3 = 13
    B. 13 - 2 = 10
    C. 10 - 4 = 7
    D. 18 - 9 = 9

1.OA.D.7

6. ◆ = 17

    ◆ could ONLY be...

    A. 17 - 5
    B. 5 + 6
    C. 19 - 2
    D. 10 + 2

1.OA.D.7

TIP of the DAY

This week is all about the equal sign. When we set two numbers equal to each other, it means they both are the same in value.

1. There are pens and pencils on the desk. The number of pens equals the number of pencils. There are 12 pencils. How many pens are there?

There are _____ pens on the desk.

1.OA.D.7

4. Which of the following statements is FALSE?

A. 10 - 2 = 7
B. 15 + 5 = 20
C. 7 + 7 = 14
D. 13 - 4 = 9

1.OA.D.7

2. 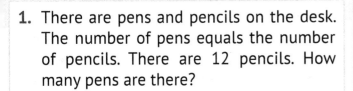 ◆ = 13

◆ could ONLY be...

A. 3 + 7
B. 10 + 3
C. 9 + 2
D. 19 - 3

1.OA.D.7

5. ■ = 19 + 1

■ could ONLY be...

A. 18 - 2
B. 15 + 5
C. 7 + 3
D. 9 - 2

1.OA.D.7

3. Which of the following statements is TRUE?

A. 9 - 2 = 6
B. 19 - 9 = 10
C. 8 - 3 = 4
D. 5 + 2 = 8

1.OA.D.7

6. ◣ = 15 - 4

◣ could ONLY be...

A. 10 + 3
B. 12 + 8
C. 7 - 2
D. 6 + 5

1.OA.D.7

TIP of the DAY

Look at this number statement and fill the blank to make it true.

15 = ___

51

WEEK 7 : DAY 5

1. Which of the following statements is TRUE?

   A. $17 + 2 = 19$
   B. $13 - 4 = 8$
   C. $4 + 3 = 6$
   D. $11 - 2 = 8$

1.OA.D.7

4. Michael bought blue and red balloons for the party. The number of blue balloons is equal to the number of red balloons Michael bought. There are 12 red balloons. How many blue balloons did Michael buy?

Michael bought _____ blue balloons.

1.OA.D.7

2. Which of the following statements is FALSE?

   A. $14 - 4 = 10$
   B. $7 + 4 = 11$
   C. $10 - 2 = 7$
   D. $19 + 1 = 20$

1.OA.D.7

5. ◆ $= 2$

   ◆ could ONLY be ...

   A. $10 - 8$
   B. $4 + 1$
   C. $2 + 1$
   D. $5 - 2$

1.OA.D.7

3. ● $= 4 + 3$

   ● could ONLY be ...

   A. $3 + 2$
   B. $10 - 3$
   C. $1 + 3$
   D. $10 - 1$

1.OA.D.7

6. Which of the following statements is FALSE?

   A. $1 + 2 = 3$
   B. $19 - 3 = 16$
   C. $10 - 2 = 7$
   D. $11 + 9 = 20$

1.OA.D.7

DAY 6
Challenge qvestion

Create your own number sentence that is true.
For example : $7 + 6 = 13$

_____ + _____ = _____

1.OA.D.7

52

VIDEO
EXPLANATIONS
ARGOPREP.COM

In Week 8 we will figure out an unknown number when we add or subtract three whole numbers.

You can find detailed video explanations of each problem in the book by visiting: ArgoPrep.com

1. Determine the unknown whole number:

$$8 + \underline{\hspace{1cm}} = 13$$

A. 3
B. 4
C. 5
D. 6

1.OA.D.8

2. What is the missing number in the equation $17 - \underline{\hspace{1cm}} = 10$?

A. 6
B. 7
C. 5
D. 8

1.OA.D.8

3. How many flowers are there in a box?

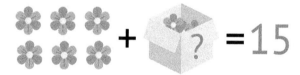

A. 4
B. 6
C. 8
D. 9

1.OA.D.8

4. Determine the unknown whole number:

$$\underline{\hspace{1cm}} + 7 = 13$$

A. 5
B. 6
C. 7
D. 8

1.OA.D.8

5. How many cats went away?

$$12 \text{ cats} - ? = 4 \text{ cats}$$

Answer: _____ cats

1.OA.D.8

6. What is $17 - 3 = \underline{\hspace{1cm}}$?

A. 15
B. 14
C. 13
D. 12

1.OA.D.8

TIP of the DAY

Use marbles to help you visualize subtraction.

1. Determine the unknown whole number:

_____ - 8 = 9

A. 20
B. 19
C. 18
D. 17

1.OA.D.8

2. Rebecca has a total of 18 balloons. Rebecca has 6 red balloons and the rest of the balloons are blue. How many blue balloons does Rebecca have?

$+ \, ? = 18$

A. 11   C. 13
B. 12   D. 14

1.OA.D.8

3. Determine the unknown whole number

12 + _____ = 19?

A. 5
B. 6
C. 7
D. 8

1.OA.D.8

4. How many squares are shaded in?

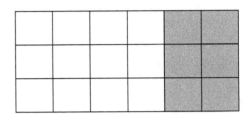

Answer: _____ squares

1.OA.D.8

5. What is 15 - 8 = _____?

A. 4
B. 5
C. 6
D. 7

1.OA.D.8

6. What is the missing number in the equation 14 = 11 + _____ ?

A. 2
B. 3
C. 4
D. 5

1.OA.D.8

TIP of the DAY

The plug and check method is a helpful strategy when you are stuck on a multiple choice problem. Do you know the plug and check method?

1. How many lollipops do you need to take away to get 9 lollipops?

$- ? = 9$

A. 1   **C.** 3
B. 2   **D.** 4

1.OA.D.8

2. Zachary and Henry have 12 apples in total. Zachary has 5 apples. How many apples does Henry have?

$- = ?$

Answer: _____ apples   1.OA.D.8

3. Determine the unknown whole number

$$14 = \text{_____} + 6?$$

A. 8
B. 7
C. 6
D. 5

1.OA.D.8

4. What is the missing number in the equation 16 - _____ = 8?

A. 9
B. 8
C. 7
D. 6

1.OA.D.8

5. How many birds flew away?

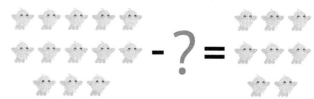

$- ? =$

A. 2
B. 3
C. 4
D. 5

1.OA.D.8

6. What is the missing number in the equation 13 + _____ = 19

Answer: _____

1.OA.D.8

TIP of the DAY

When you don't understand a question, draw a box around the question so you can ask your teacher or parent for help.

1. There are 12 pencils in a box. How many pencils should be added to have 18 of them?

 $+\ ?\ =\ 18$

Answer: _____ pencils

1.OA.D.8

2. What is the missing number in the equation _____ = 11 - 4?

A. 8
B. 7
C. 6
D. 5

1.OA.D.8

3. Determine the unknown whole number

$$3 + \text{_____} = 15$$

A. 10
B. 11
C. 12
D. 13

1.OA.D.8

4. There were 5 black rabbits, 3 white rabbits and some brown rabbits. The total number of rabbits is 11. How many brown rabbits are there?

 $+\ ?\ =\ 11$

A. 2
B. 3
C. 4
D. 5

1.OA.D.8

5. What is the missing number in the equation 7 + ___ = 16.

Answer: _____

1.OA.D.8

6. Enter a number in the box to make the number sentence true.

$$\text{_____} + 6 = 11$$

1.OA.D.8

TIP *of the* **DAY**

The more you keep practicing these types of questions, you will develop a stronger sense of mental math calculations. Keep up the great work!

1. Fourteen fish were bought and placed in two aquariums. There are 6 fish in the first aquarium. How many fish are there in the second aquarium?

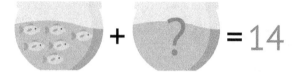

   A. 9
   B. 8
   C. 7
   D. 6

   1.OA.D.8

2. Determine the unknown whole number:

   $$15 - \underline{\hspace{2cm}} = 6?$$

   A. 9
   B. 8
   C. 7
   D. 6

   1.OA.D.8

3. Fill in the box to make the number sentence true.

   $$\underline{\hspace{2cm}} + 7 = 11$$

   1.OA.D.8

4. There are 12 benches at the playground. Five of them are green and the other benches are yellow. How many yellow benches are there at the playground?

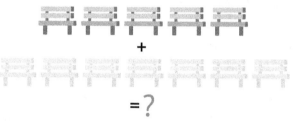

   Answer: _____

   1.OA.D.8

5. Determine the unknown whole number:

   $$\underline{\hspace{2cm}} = 18 - 7$$

   A. 10
   B. 11
   C. 12
   D. 13

   1.OA.D.8

6. Kollin thought of the number which when added to 8 gives 15. Which number did Kollin think of?

   A. 4
   B. 5
   C. 6
   D. 7

   1.OA.D.8

DAY 6

Challenge qvestion

Determine the unknown whole number in this equation to make it equal.

$$6 + 13 = 8 + \underline{\hspace{2cm}}$$

1.OA.D.8

WEEK 9

In Week 9 we get down to some serious business! We will count to the number 120.
You can find detailed video explanations of each problem in the book by visiting:
ArgoPrep.com

WEEK 9 : DAY 1

1. Complete the number pattern:

_____ 1,845   1,855   1,865

A. 1,825
B. 1,835
C. 1,836
D. 1,875

1.NBT.A.1

2. What number does the model show?

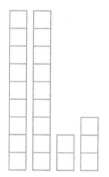

A. 22   C. 24
B. 23   D. 25

1.NBT.A.1

3. How do you write the number 3 and 4 in words? Select the correct answer choice.

A. Two and Nine
B. Three and Four
C. Ten and One
D. Seven and Eight

1.NBT.A.1

4. Which picture shows 20 apples?

A.

B.

C.

D.

1.NBT.A.1

5. Find the missing number and write it in the box below.

1	2	3	4	5	6	7	8	9	10
11	12	13	14	15	16	17	18	19	20
21	22	23	24	25	26	27	28	29	30
31	32	33	34	35	36	37	38	39	40
41	42	43		45	46	47	48	49	50
51	52	53	54	55	56	57	58	59	60
61	62	63	64	65	66	67	68	69	70
71	72	73	74	75	76	77	78	79	80
81	82	83	84	85	86	87	88	89	90
91	92	93	94	95	96	97	98	99	100

_____

1.NBT.A.1

TIP of the DAY

Solving a pattern question can be very fun! Carefully look for the pattern that is happening to each number. 4, 6, 8, ? You can tell that each number increases by 2. Therefore, to solve for the missing number, we can add the number 8 by 2 to get 10.

1. How many cookies do you see?

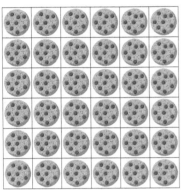

A. 20   C. 36
B. 35   D. 40   1.NBT.A.1

2. Count how many dogs you see on the picture and then select the correct answer choice.

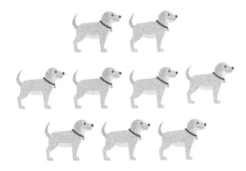

A. Eight
B. Nine
C. Ten
D. Eleven   1.NBT.A.1

3. Count by ones or tens to find the sum:

$$45 + 5 = \boxed{}$$

A. 47
B. 49
C. 50
D. 70   1.NBT.A.1

4. Which addition sentence does the picture below show?

A. 3 + 3 = 6
B. 4 + 2 = 5
C. 4 + 3 = 7
D. 4 + 3 = 5   1.NBT.A.1

5. If you take the number 9 and add it to the number 10, what number will you have?

A. 17
B. 19
C. 29
D. 39   1.NBT.A.1

TIP of the DAY

Let's continue playing the game "I am thinking of a number..."
I am thinking of a number that equals 8 when it is added to 1. What is the number

1. Count the number of circles on the picture and write your answer in the text box below.

_____

1.NBT.A.1

2. Starting at 80, count forward the next 8 numbers, what will you get?

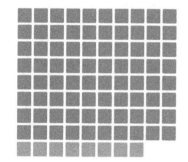

A. 79
B. 87
C. 88
D. 90

1.NBT.A.1

3. What is the total number of fruits in the picture below?

A. 6
B. 4
C. 3
D. 2

1.NBT.A.1

4. What is the total number of animals shown in the pictures below?

A. 8
B. 9
C. 12
D. 15

1.NBT.A.1

5. What number does the model below show?

A. 20
B. 22
C. 23
D. 25

1.NBT.A.1

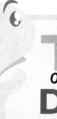

TIP
of the
DAY

Practicing your math skills only 15 minutes a day at your home will greatly benefit you in the long run!

62

1. Count by tens and find the sum of.

$$20 + 80 + 10 = \boxed{}$$

A. 100
B. 105
C. 110
D. 120

1.NBT.A.1

2. Which addition sentence does the picture below show?

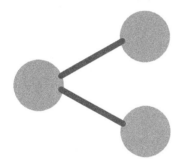

A. 1 + 1 = 2
C. 3 + 1 = 4
B. 1 + 2 = 3
D. 2 + 2 = 4

1.NBT.A.1

3. Complete the number pattern and write your answer in the text box below:

4,000 4,010 _____ 4,030

_____

1.NBT.A.1

4. How many stars are shown in the picture given below?

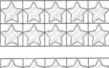

A. 40
C. 60
B. 50
D. 75

1.NBT.A.1

5. How many cars are shown in the picture below. Count by fives or ones and find the sum.

A. 15
C. 17
B. 16
D. 20

1.NBT.A.1

TIP of the DAY

Let's count by fives! Count to the number 100 in groups of 5. Here are the first few numbers to get you started. 5, 10, 15, 20, 25, 30... Finish the rest, you can do it!

1. Look at the image. Find the two missing numbers, then sum them up and write your answer in the text box below:

1		3	4	5	6	7		9	10
11	12	13	14	15	16	17	18	19	20
21	22	23	24	25	26	27	28	29	30
31	32	33	34	35	36	37	38	39	40
41	42	43	44	45	46	47	48	49	50
51	52	53	54	55	56	57	58	59	60
61	62	63	64	65	66	67	68	69	70
71	72	73	74	75	76	77	78	79	80
81	82	83	84	85	86	87	88	89	90
91	92	93	94	95	96	97	98	99	100

_____

1.NBT.A.1

2. Count the number of tally marks, then add the number 5. Choose the number that you got.

A. 18   C. 27
B. 22   D. 30

1.NBT.A.1

3. Count by ones or tens to find the sum: 43 + 35 =

A. 76   C. 78
B. 77   D. 90

1.NBT.A.1

4. Count by fives or tens to find the sum:

$$20 + 45 + 5 =$$

A. 50
B. 55
C. 60
D. 70

1.NBT.A.1

5. Count by ones, fives or tens to find the sum: 30 + 35 + 5 + 50 =

A. 70
B. 80
C. 115
D. 120

1.NBT.A.1

6. How many shapes are colored in below?

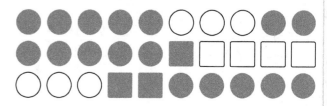

A. 11
B. 17
C. 19
D. 20

1.NBT.A.1

DAY 6

Challenge qvestion

Count by ones, fives or tens to find the sum:
20 + 22 + 21 + 25
Write your answer in the text box below:

_____

1.NBT.A.1

WEEK 10

VIDEO EXPLANATIONS

ARGOPREP.COM

Week 10 is all about understanding two digit numbers and learning about the tens and ones place value.

You can find detailed video explanations of each problem in the book by visiting: ArgoPrep.com

1. Count the number of tens and ones below.

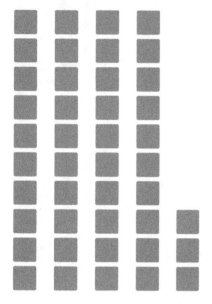

There are _____ tens

There are _____ ones

1.NBT.B.2

2. In the number 33, there are:

A. 4 tens and 3 ones

B. 3 ones and 3 tens

C. 3 ones and 2 tens

D. 3 tens and 2 ones

1.NBT.B.2

3. Count the stars and choose the correct answer.

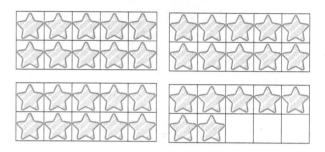

A. 3 tens + 7 ones = 37

B. 4 tens + 2 ones - 42

C. 2 tens + 9 ones = 29

D. 3 tens + 8 ones = 38

1.NBT.B.2

4. Read the information given and choose the correct answer choice.

This number is greater than 66.

This number is less than 70.

It has 8 ones.

A. 67   C. 78

B. 68   D. 88

1.NBT.B.2

5. Look at the expression and write the missing number in the text box below.

68 = 6 tens + ☐ ones

_____

1.NBT.B.2

TIP of the DAY

Let's count by tens! Count to the number 100 in groups of 10. Here are the first few numbers to get you started. 10, 20, 30 ... Finish the rest, you can do it!

1. The number 90 has 9 tens and 0 ones. What is another way to make the number 90?

   A. 8 tens + 10 ones
   B. 7 tens + 9 ones
   C. 5 ones + 5 tens
   D. 6 tens + 20 ones

1.NBT.B.2

2. Jeremy baked 45 cookies. How can I put the cookies by groups? Write your answer below:

   _____ tens + _____ ones = 45

1.NBT.B.2

3. Complete each equation below.

   A. 6 + ____ = 10
   B. 30 + _____ = 50
   C. 50 + _____ = 50
   D. 10 + _____ = 18

1.NBT.B.2

4. Look at the picture. Count the clouds.

   How many tens? _____
   How many ones? _____
   How many clouds? _____

1.NBT.B.2

5. Which answer choice below represents the number 120?

   A. 10 tens+ 20 ones
   B. 11 tens + 0 ones
   C. 10 tens + 10 ones
   D. 120 ones + 2 tens

1.NBT.B.2

TIP of the DAY

When counting items in a picture, it is helpful to group them in boxes so you can keep track.

1. How many raspberries are there?
   Note: Each raspberry drawn represents 10 raspberries

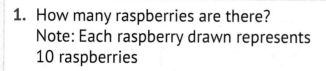

   A. 7   C. 77
   B. 70   D. 0   1.NBT.B.2

2. How many tens are in the number 79?

   A. 6
   B. 7
   C. 8
   D. 9   1.NBT.B.2

3. Count the bananas. How many tens are there?

   A. 2 tens   C. 4 tens
   B. 3 tens   D. 5 tens   1.NBT.B.2

4. Read the clue below and then choose the correct answer choice:
   Tom's age is less than 19, but greater than 10 and it has 5 ones. How old is Tom?

   A. 14 years old
   B. 15 years old
   C. 18 years old
   D. 25 years old   1.NBT.B.2

5. Look at the picture below. Count the number of oranges.

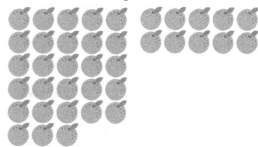

   A. 38   C. 48
   B. 43   D. 50   1.NBT.B.2

6. Using the picture above in question 5, what is another way to write the number of oranges?

   A. 1 ten plus 18 ones
   B. 1 ten plus 28 ones
   C. 38 ones plus 10 tens
   D. 18 ones and 1 ten   1.NBT.B.2

TIP of the DAY

When working with word problems, always underline the keywords that tell you how to solve the problem.

1. Regroup the following expression.

Note: write a number from 0 to 9 in each box.

6 tens + 12 ones =

☐ tens ☐ + ones

1.NBT.B.2

2. Count the dots below and choose the correct answer choice.

A. 1 ten + 7 ones
B. 1 one + 0 tens
C. 2 tens + 0 ones
D. 0 tens + 8 ones

1.NBT.B.2

3. Complete each equation below.

A. 3 + _____ = 33
B. 6 + _____ = 60
C. 90 + _____ = 100
D. 105 + _____ = 120

1.NBT.B.2

4. Which equation represents the model shown below?

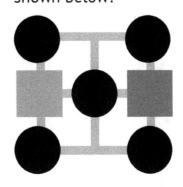

A. 5 ones + 2 ones
B. 7 tens + 2 ones
C. 7 ones + 4 tens
D. 5 ones + 5 ones

1.NBT.B.2

5. How many tens are in the number 120?

A. 6
B. 12
C. 11
D. 0

1.NBT.B.2

6. In the number 119, there are:

A. 11 tens and 10 ones
B. 11 tens and 9 ones
C. 9 ones and 10 tens
D. 3 tens and 9 ones

1.NBT.B.2

Always check the sign to determine if you will be adding to find the sum or subtracting to find the difference.

1. What equation represents the model shown below?

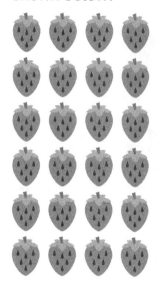

A. 3 tens + 4 ones
B. 2 tens + 4 ones
C. 3 tens + 3 ones
D. 2 ones + 4 tens

1.NBT.B.2

2. Read the information given and choose the correct answer choice.

This number is greater than 23
This number is less than 30
It has 7 ones.

A. 17   C. 28
B. 27   D. 37

1.NBT.B.2

3. Which answer choice below represents the number 96

A. 9 tens 6 ones
B. 9 ones + 6 tens
C. 9 tens + 0 ones
D. 9 tens + 9 ones

1.NBT.B.2

4. Count the stars and choose the correct answer.

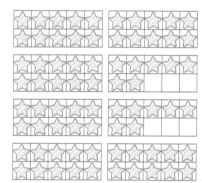

A. 7 tens + 4 ones
B. 7 tens + 5 ones
C. 8 tens + 4 ones
D. 8 tens + 2 ones

1.NBT.B.2

5. Regroup the following expression.

Note: write a number from 0 to 9 in each box.

7 tens + 18 ones = tens ☐ + ones ☐

1.NBT.B.2

DAY 6
Challenge qvestion

What will be the number if it has
4 tens + 6 ones + 2 tens + 5 tens?

_____

1.NBT.B.2

WEEK 11

VIDEO EXPLANATIONS ▷ ARGOPREP.COM

Get ready to compare two digit numbers in Week 11. Which number is greater: 10 or 20? You will have the opportunity to practice lots of numbers and compare their values.

You can find detailed video explanations of each problem in the book by visiting:
ArgoPrep.com

1. Which words make this statement true?

20_____ 20

A. Is greater than
B. Is less than
C. Is equal to
D. Is greater than or equal to

1.NBT.B.3

2. Fill in the blank.

60_____40

A. <
B. >
C. =
D. ≤

1.NBT.B.3

3. Michael bought 3 cookies. Jessica had 10 cookies. Who has more cookies?

A. Michael
B. Jessica
C. Michael and Jessica have the same amount of cookies.

1.NBT.B.3

4. Look at the number sequences below and choose from greatest to least.

A. 99, 43, 11, 33
B. 85, 44, 82, 90
C. 99, 80, 34, 11
D. 11, 70, 45, 90

1.NBT.B.3

5. Look at the number sequences below and choose from least to greatest.

A. 4, 8, 19, 0
B. 18, 32, 17, 20
C. 110, 77, 33, 23
D. 12, 17, 58, 97

1.NBT.B.3

6. Which of the following numbers is greater than 46?

A. 5
B. 50
C. 33
D. 46

1.NBT.B.3

TIP
of the
DAY

Always double check your work!

1. Christine is in 4th grade. John is three years older than Christine. What grade is John in?

   A. 3rd grade
   B. 4th grade
   C. 5th grade
   D. 7th grade

   1.NBT.B.3

2. Anna has 2 cats. Eduard has twice as many cats as Anna and a dog. How many animals does Eduard have?

   A. 3
   B. 4
   C. 5
   D. 6

   1.NBT.B.3

3. Paul collected 67 marbles in a game. Caroline collected the same amount of marbles. How many marbles does Caroline have?

   A. 55
   B. 66
   C. 67
   D. Cannot be determined.

   1.NBT.B.3

4. Which words make this statement true?

   73_____ 20

   A. Is greater than
   B. Is less than
   C. Is equal to
   D. Is greater than or equal to

   1.NBT.B.3

5. Team A won 4 games. Team B lost 4 games. Team C has won the same amount of games as Team A. Choose the correct statement below.

   A. Team A = Team C = Team B
   B. Team A = Team C > Team B
   C. Team B < Team C < Team A
   D. Team B ≥ Team C ≤ Team A

   1.NBT.B.3

6. Look at the number sequences below and choose the correct one.

   A. 22 > 12
   B. 44 = 55
   C. 17 > 18
   D. 8 > 9

   1.NBT.B.3

TIP *of the* **DAY**

Remember your three important comparison symbols.
  = Equal Sign
  > Greater than sign
  < Less than sign

1. Compare the two pictures below.

There are more _____ than bananas.

1.NBT.B.3

2. Fill in the blank to make the statements true.

45 is greater than _____.

57 is equal to _____

14 is less than _____.

1.NBT.B.3

3. David is 8 years old. In 3 months he will be 9 years old. Juliana is 3 years younger than David. In 3 months, how old will Juliana be?

A. 5 years old
B. 6 years old
C. Same as David
D. Cannot be found

1.NBT.B.3

4. Count the squares and circles. How many more circles are there than squares?

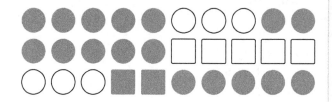

A. 16
B. 15
C. 17
D. 0

1.NBT.B.3

5. In June there are 30 days. In July there are 31 days. In August there are 31 days. Choose **all** correct statements below.

A. June = July = August
B. August > June
C. July > June
D. July < June = August

1.NBT.B.3

6. Which of the following numbers are greater than 23 but less than 30?

A. 5, 6, 90
B. 24, 26, 29
C. 33, 24, 60
D. 22, 24, 28

1.NBT.B.3

TIP of the DAY

When reading a pictograph, be sure to check the key to see what one picture is equal to.

1. Harvey found 10 butterflies. Mike has 3 more. Jessica has 6 fewer than Mike and Harvey together. How many butterflies does Jessica have?

   A. 13   C. 17

   B. 16   D. 18

   1.NBT.B.3

2. Look at the picture shown below. Compare the number of stars, squares and circles. Which of the following shows the correct statement.

   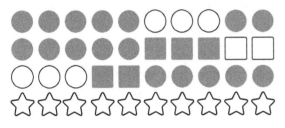

   A. Stars < Squares < Circles

   B. Squares = Stars > Circles

   C. Circles > Stars > Squares

   D. Circles = Stars = Squares

   1.NBT.B.3

3. Fill in the blank using the comparison symbols (<, > , =)

   12_____40_____55

   1.NBT.B.3

4. Fill in the blank to make the statements true.

   22 is greater than _____.

   67 is equal to _____.

   99 is less than _____.

   1.NBT.B.3

5. Which words make this statement true?

   11_____ 20

   A. Is greater than

   B. Is less than

   C. Is equal to

   D. Is greater than or equal to

   1.NBT.B.3

6. Phillip scored 16 points in total for the two games. His sister Paula scored 3 points fewer than Philip for the two games. Which statement is true?

   A. Paula scored 19 points.

   B. Paula scored 13 points.

   C. Paula and Phillip scored the same points.

   D. Cannot be determined.

   1.NBT.B.3

TIP of the DAY

Confused with the comparison signs < and > ? Here's a fun way to remember the greater than sign >. The greater than sign looks like an alligator mouth opening wide!

1. In the picture shown below, which 2 figures appear the most often?

   A. Heart and Star
   B. Heart and Square
   C. Start and Circle
   D. Heart

   1.NBT.B.3

2. Carl is two years older than Marry. Marry is the same age as John. In 4 months John will be 2 years old. How old will Carl be in 4 months?

   A. 2 years old   C. 5 years old
   B. 4 years old   D. 6 years old

   1.NBT.B.3

3. Choose the answer choice that is NOT correct.

   A. 45 > 32 = 32
   B. 27 < 34 > 27
   C. 97 < 98 < 99
   D. 12 > 13 < 12

   1.NBT.B.3

4. Fill in the blank to make the statements true.

   2 is greater than _____.

   45 is equal to _____.

   28 is less than _____.   1.NBT.B.3

5. Look at the number sequences below and choose the correct one.

   A. 98 > 89
   B. 21 = 55
   C. 16 < 11
   D. 57 < 47

   1.NBT.B.3

6. Look at the picture below and find the number of cats and number of dogs. Compare and choose the correct answer choice.

   A. 8 < 9   C. 10 = 10
   B. 9 < 10   D. 3 > 1

   1.NBT.B.3

DAY 6
Challenge qvestion

Jonathan has 10 pencils. His sister has 3 pencils more than Robert. Robert has 3 fewer pencils than Jonathan. How many pencils does Jonathan's sister have?

_____

1.NBT.B.3

WEEK 12

VIDEO EXPLANATIONS ▶ ARGOPREP.COM

In Week 12, we will add and subtract within 100 using models and drawings.

You can find detailed video explanations of each problem in the book by visiting:
ArgoPrep.com

1. Which of the following answer choices equal to 55 + 13 = ?

   A. 67
   B. 68
   C. 70
   D. 71

1.NBT.C.4

2. 87 is 8 tens plus 7 ones. What is another way to make 87?

   A. 6 tens 18 ones
   B. 6 tens 19 ones
   C. 7 tens 17 ones
   D. 7 tens 18 ones

1.NBT.C.4

3. Write the addition sentence that the model below shows.

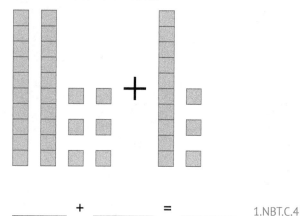

_____ + _____ = _____

1.NBT.C.4

4. Gregory has 42 kg of potato. Hillary has 30 kg of carrot. Count by ones or tens to find how many kg of vegetable they have together.

   A. 70 kg
   B. 71 kg
   C. 72 kg
   D. 73 kg

1.NBT.C.4

5. Regroup the given equation below. Write a number from 0 to 9 in each box.

   5 tens + 13 ones =

   ☐ tens + ☐ ones

1.NBT.C.4

6. Look at the picture below. Count by ones or tens. How many tvs are there in total?

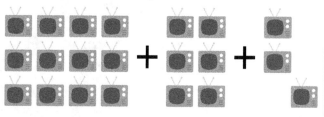

   A. 20
   B. 21
   C. 22
   D. 25

1.NBT.C.4

TIP of the DAY

Regrouping allows us to change the groups of ones and tens to make adding or subtracting easier.

1. Anton went to Summer Camp. There were 17 boys, excluding Anton, and 20 girls. How many kids were in Summer Camp?

A. 37
B. 38
C. 40
D. 47

1.NBT.C.4

2. On the picture below you can see the total number of phones. If you add 10 more, how many will you have? Count by ones or tens and write your answer below.

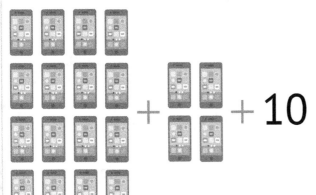

_____

1.NBT.C.4

3. Add 49 + 21 =

A. 30
B. 67
C. 70
D. 71

1.NBT.C.4

4. Choose the correct addition sentence that the model below shows.

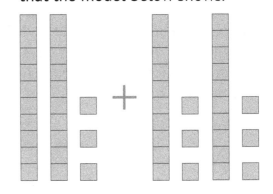

A. 23 + 26 = 49
B. 23 + 26 = 50
C. 23 + 35 = 58
D. 21 + 22 = 43

1.NBT.C.4

5. Which of the following is equal to 88 + 12?

A. 97
B. 98
C. 99
D. 100

1.NBT.C.4

TIP
of the
DAY

Take a look at the following example: 72 + 12 =
To make this easier to calculate we can rewrite this as
72 + 10 + 2 =

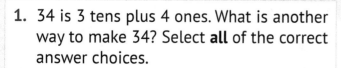

1. 34 is 3 tens plus 4 ones. What is another way to make 34? Select **all** of the correct answer choices.

   A. 2 tens 14 ones
   B. 1 tens 24 ones
   C. 0 tens 34 ones
   D. 3 tens 5 ones

   1.NBT.C.4

2. Alex drove 45 miles on Monday and 30 miles on Friday. All the other days he was not driving. How many miles in total did he drive?

   A. 3 tens + 15 ones + 3 tens = 75 ones
   B. 3 tens + 16 ones + 2 tens = 48 ones
   C. 4 tens + 5 ones + 3 ones = 48 ones
   D. 5 tens + 5 ones + 3 tens = 85 ones

   1.NBT.C.4

3. Kevin read 10 books during the summer. Jessica read 13 books more than Kevin. How many books did they read all together?

   A. 1 tens + 2 tens + 3 ones = 33 ones
   B. 1 tens + 2 tens + 3 ones = 6 tens
   C. 1 tens + 2 ones + 3 ones = 15 ones
   D. 1 tens + 5 tens + 3 ones = 63 ones

   1.NBT.C.4

4. Select **all** of the correct answer choices that the model below shows.

   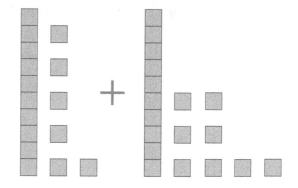

   A. 1 tens + 6 ones + 1 tens + 8 ones
   B. 1 tens + 6 ones + 18 ones
   C. 1 tens + 5 ones + 1 tens + 7 ones
   D. 16 ones + 18 ones

   1.NBT.C.4

5. Regroup the given equation below. Write a number from 0 to 9 in each box.

   2 tens + 11 ones =

   ☐ tens + ☐ ones

   1.NBT.C.4

6. Count by ones or tens to find the sum:

   56 + 32 = ?

   A. 79
   B. 80
   C. 87
   D. 88

   1.NBT.C.4

TIP of the DAY

If you have trouble regrouping numbers, use unifix cubes to help you visualize!

1. Which of the following is equal to 27 + 54?

    A. 79
    B. 80
    C. 81
    D. 82

1.NBT.C.4

2. Choose the correct addition sentence that the model below shows.

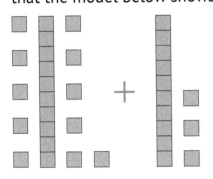

    A. 21 + 13 = 33
    B. 21 + 12 = 33
    C. 21 + 13 = 34
    D. 21 + 17 = 40

1.NBT.C.4

3. Add 17 + 37

    A. 54
    B. 44
    C. 34
    D. 24

1.NBT.C.4

4. Add 18 + 43 + 12

    A. 70
    B. 71
    C. 72
    D. 73

1.NBT.C.4

5. 7 tens + 24 ones is equal to:

    A. 84
    B. 85
    C. 94
    D. 95

1.NBT.C.4

6. Heleny went to a trip with 3 pairs of sunglasses. On the trip she bought 13 sunglasses for her friends and family. How many sunglasses does she have in total now?

    A. 16
    B. 19
    C. 20
    D. 21

1.NBT.C.4

TIP *of the* **DAY**

Take a highlighter and highlight the ones place when you solve addition problems with two digits.

Example:

$$\begin{array}{r} 25 \\ + \ 17 \\ \hline 42 \end{array}$$

1. Look at the picture below. Count by ones or tens. How many stars are there in total?

A. 19 C. 33
B. 29 D. 36

1.NBT.C.4

2. Look at the picture below. Count by ones or tens. How many stars are there in total?

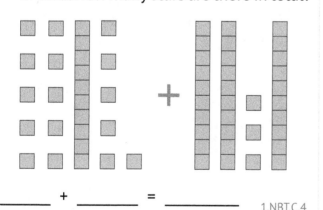

_____ + _____ = _____

1.NBT.C.4

3. Count the birds below by ones or tens and write your answer below.

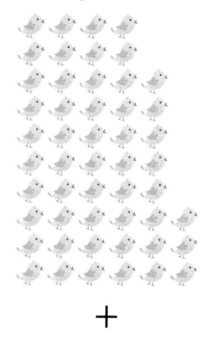

+

_____ + _____ = _____

1.NBT.C.4

DAY 6
Challenge
qvestion

Gary is 35 years old. His older brother John is 1 ten + 13 ones older. How old is John?

John is_____years old.

1.NBT.C.4

WEEK 13

VIDEO EXPLANATIONS ▶ ARGOPREP.COM

Time for some mental math in Week 13. We will practice finding 10 more or 10 less than a number mentally!

You can find detailed video explanations of each problem in the book by visiting:
ArgoPrep.com

1. What number is 10 more than 13?

   A. 22

   B. 23

   C. 24

   D. 33

1.NBT.C.5

2. What number is 10 less than the model presented below?

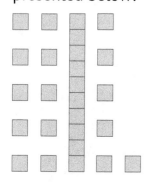

   A. 15

   B. 16

   C. 10

   D. 5

1.NBT.C.5

3. Using mental math, find the numbers that are 10 less and 10 more that the number shown below.

_____ , 76 , _____

1.NBT.C.5

4. Add 10 + 40 =

   A. 30

   B. 40

   C. 50

   D. 60

1.NBT.C.5

5. Which number will you get if you add 10 to the model shown below?

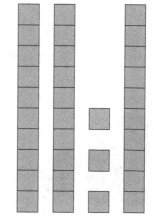

   A. 33   **C.** 53

   B. 43   **D.** 63

1.NBT.C.5

6. What number is 10 less than 13?

   A. 3

   B. 4

   C. 8

   D. 10

1.NBT.C.5

TIP of the DAY

When looking for patterns, think about how the numbers change.

1. Gaby has 7 pens in her desk. David has 10 more than Gaby. How many pens does David have?

   A. 7
   B. 10
   C. 17
   D. 18

   1.NBT.C.5

2. What number is 10 more than 65?

   A. 55
   B. 65
   C. 75
   D. 80

   1.NBT.C.5

3. Using mental math, write the numbers that are 10 less and 10 greater the number shown below.

   _____ ,31, _____

   1.NBT.C.5

4. Which of the following is equal to 10 + 10 + 32?

   A. 51
   B. 52
   C. 53
   D. 60

   1.NBT.C.5

5. What number will you get if you add 10 and then subtract 10 to the model shown below? Write your answer below.

   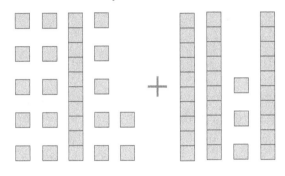

   _____

   1.NBT.C.5

6. Subtract 10 from 67.

   A. 37
   B. 47
   C. 57
   D. 67

   1.NBT.C.5

TIP of the DAY

Circle keywords or actions in word problems. Re-read your word problem to see if there are keywords to help you solve it.

1. Jessica and Mike ate a total of 5 burgers. Samantha ate 2 burgers. How many burgers in total were eaten?

A. 13
B. 9
C. 7
D. 5

1.NBT.C.5

2. What number is 10 more than 68 and 10 less than 88?

A. 68
B. 78
C. 88
D. 98

1.NBT.C.5

3. What number is 10 more than the model? Write your answer below.

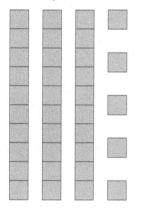

_____

1.NBT.C.5

4. Using mental math, write the numbers that are 10 less and 10 greater the number shown below.

_____ , 73 , _____

1.NBT.C.5

5. What numbers are 10 less than 14 and 10 more than 4?

A. 3 and 4
B. 4 and 14
C. 5 and 14
D. 8 and 5

1.NBT.C.5

6. Heleny has $18. Margaret paid Heleny $10 for babysitting. Then Heleny spent $3. How much money does Heleny have now?

A. $18
B. $20
C. $25
D. $27

1.NBT.C.5

TIP
of the
DAY

The more you practice your math skills, the faster you will be able to mentally calculate numbers.

1. Which number is 10 more than the model below?

+ 10

   A. 27
   C. 29
   B. 28
   D. 30

1.NBT.C.5

2. Which of the following equations is **NOT** correct?

   A. 10 + 48 + 10 = 68
   B. 40 + 10 + 10 = 60
   C. 10 - 10 + 10 = 10
   D. 3 + 10 - 3 = 3

1.NBT.C.5

3. What number is 10 more than 24?

   A. 24
   B. 25
   C. 34
   D. 35

1.NBT.C.5

4. Which number is 10 less than the model shown below?

   A. 6
   B. 16
   C. 26
   D. 27

1.NBT.C.5

5. Which of the following equations is correct?

   A. 33 + 10 - 3 = 13
   B. 45 - 10 + 10 = 45
   C. 7 + 10 + 7 = 25
   D. 99 - 10 + 4 = 78

1.NBT.C.5

 TIP *of the* DAY

Another great tip to increase your mental math skills is to speed solve basic addition and subtraction problems.

1. Which number does the model below show?

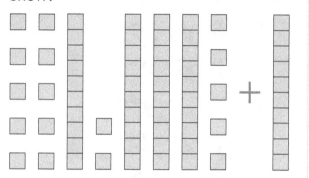

A. 66
B. 67
C. 68
D. 78

1.NBT.C.5

3. Which number does the model show below?

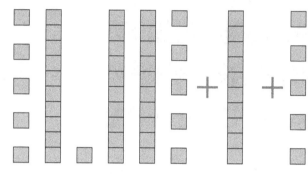

A. 55
B. 56
C. 57
D. 58

1.NBT.C.5

2. Using mental math, write the numbers that are 10 less and 10 greater the number shown below.

_____ , 44, _____

1.NBT.C.5

4. Gregory and Melony are playing basketball. In the first round Melony scored 10 points more than Gregory, but 10 less than Gregory in the second round. If Gregory scored 4 points the first round and 14 points the second round, what is the total points Melony scored?

A. 10 points
B. 14 points
C. 18 points
D. 20 points

1.NBT.C.5

DAY 6
Challenge qvestion

Using mental math, write the two numbers that are 10 less and 10 greater than the number shown below.

_____, 20, _____

1.NBT.C.5

WEEK 14

VIDEO EXPLANATIONS ▶ ARGOPREP.COM

In Week 14, we will subtract multiples of 10 using models and drawings.

You can find detailed video explanations of each problem in the book by visiting:
ArgoPrep.com

1. What is 50 - 10?

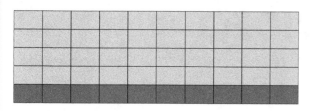

A. 4   **C.** 40

B. 30   **D.** 10

1.NBT.C.6

2. Which number sentence matches the picture?

A. 6 - 2 = 8

B. 60 - 2 = 80

C. 60 - 2 = 8

D. 60 - 20 = 40

1.NBT.C.6

3. 80 - 60 =

A. 40

B. 30

C. 20

D. 10

1.NBT.C.6

4. The picture shows 30 + 20. What is 50 - 20?

A. 10

B. 20

C. 30

D. 40

1.NBT.C.6

5. What is 80 - 40?

A. 20

B. 40

C. 50

D. 60

1.NBT.C.6

6. The ribbon is 60 inches in length. A 20-inch piece of this ribbon is cut off. What is the new length of the ribbon? _____ inches

1.NBT.C.6

TIP of the DAY

Using visual diagrams can help you solve and understand the question better. Always use the pictures provided to help you.

1. Which number sentence matches the picture?

- **A.** 70 - 3 = 4
- **B.** 70 - 4 = 3
- **C.** 70 - 40 = 30
- **D.** 70 - 30 = 40

1.NBT.C.6

2. 30 + 60 = 90. What is 90 - 60?

- **A.** 20
- **B.** 30
- **C.** 40
- **D.** 50

1.NBT.C.6

3. What is 80 - 70?

- **A.** 10
- **B.** 20
- **C.** 30
- **D.** 40

1.NBT.C.6

4. What is 90 - 50?

- **A.** 30
- **B.** 40
- **C.** 50
- **D.** 60

1.NBT.C.6

5. Which equation equals 60 - 20?

- **A.** 20 + 60
- **B.** 40 + 60
- **C.** 20 - 40
- **D.** 20 + 20

1.NBT.C.6

6. Matthew had 70 cents. He spent 20 cents. How much money does Matthew have now?

_____ cents

1.NBT.C.6

TIP of the DAY

This week we are learning how to subtract in multiples of 10. Let's try this pattern that is subtracting the previous number by 10.

90 , 80 , 70 , 60 , ...

Finish the pattern until you get to 0

1. If there were 50 swans and 30 swans flew away, how many swans remain?

- **A.** 10
- **B.** 20
- **C.** 30
- **D.** 40

1.NBT.C.6

2. Look at the picture. What is 80 - 20?

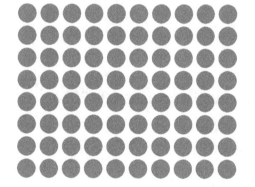

Answer: _____

1.NBT.C.6

3. What is 90 - 60?

- **A.** 10
- **B.** 20
- **C.** 30
- **D.** 40

1.NBT.C.6

4. 10 + 30 = 40. What is 40 - 30?

- **A.** 10
- **B.** 20
- **C.** 30
- **D.** 40

1.NBT.C.6

5. Which number sentence matches the picture?

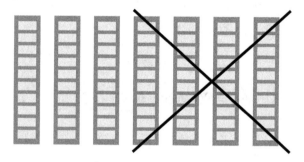

- **A.** 80 - 30 = 50
- **B.** 80 - 40 = 40
- **C.** 70 - 30 = 40
- **D.** 70 - 40 = 30

1.NBT.C.6

6. There were 50 apples on the apple tree. Ten apples fell on the ground. How many apples remain on the apple tree?

_____ apples

1.NBT.C.6

TIP of the DAY

Since we are learning how to subtract by 10, we should also know how to add by 10. Let's try this pattern that is adding the previous number by 10.

20 , 30 , 40 , 50 , 60 .....

Finish the pattern until you get to 90.

1. 50 + 40 = 90. What is 90 - 40?

   A. 30
   B. 40
   C. 50
   D. 60

   1.NBT.C.6

2. There are 30 total green and yellow parrots at the pet-shop. 10 of the parrots are green. How many yellow parrots are there at the pet-shop?

   _____ yellow parrots

   1.NBT.C.6

3. Which number sentence is equivalent to 40 + 30 = 70?

   A. 50 - 30 = 20
   B. 60 - 30 = 30
   C. 70 - 30 = 40
   D. 90 - 30 = 60

   1.NBT.C.6

4. Which number sentence is shown in the picture?
   Note: Each pear drawn represents 10 pears.

   A. 60 - 50 = 10
   B. 70 - 50 = 20
   C. 80 - 30 = 50
   D. 70 - 40 = 30

   1.NBT.C.6

5. There were 60 cars in the parking lot. Then 30 cars drove away. How many cars were left in the parking lot?

   A. 10
   B. 20
   C. 30
   D. 40

   1.NBT.C.6

6. There were 90 balloons in the party. Amy took 20 balloons home. How many balloons remain in the party?

   A. 70   C. 50
   B. 60   D. 40

   1.NBT.C.6

TIP of the DAY

It is very helpful when you underline the keywords that tell you whether or not you need to add or subtract. Since we are only working on subtraction this week, go ahead and underline all the keywords in each problem that tell us this is a subtraction problem.

1. There were 60 balls in the basket. Ten balls were put into another basket. How many balls are there in the first basket now?

   A. 20
   B. 30
   C. 40
   D. 50

   1.NBT.C.6

2. The picture shows 10 + 80. What is 90 - 80?

   A. 10
   B. 20
   C. 30
   D. 40

   1.NBT.C.6

3. What is 30 - 20?

   Answer: _____

   1.NBT.C.6

4. What is the missing number in the equation

   $$80 - _____ = 50?$$

   A. 10
   B. 20
   C. 30
   D. 40

   1.NBT.C.6

5. There were 70 people at a railway station. After the train left only 30 people remained. How many people entered the train?

   _____ people

   1.NBT.C.6

6. What is 60 - 20 - 10?

   A. 50
   B. 40
   C. 30
   D. 20

   1.NBT.C.6

DAY 6
Challenge qvestion

What is the missing number in the equation

$$20 + 50 = 90 - _____$$

1.NBT.C.6

94

WEEK 15

Week 15 is super fun! We will order three objects by length. You will order the objects shortest to largest or the other way around.

You can find detailed video explanations of each problem in the book by visiting:
ArgoPrep.com

1. Put the musical instruments in order from the shortest to the longest.

- **A.** The violin, the grand synthesizer, the guitar
- **B.** The guitar, the violin, the grand synthesizer
- **C.** The grand synthesizer, the violin, the guitar
- **D.** The violin, the guitar, the grand synthesizer

1.MD.A.1

2. Put the animals in order from the longest to the shortest.

- **A.** Dog, hare, mouse.
- **B.** Hare, dog, mouse.
- **C.** Mouse, dog, hare.
- **D.** Dog, mouse, hare.

1.MD.A.1

3. Put the flowers in order from the longest to shortest.

- **A.** 1, 2, 3
- **B.** 2, 3, 1
- **C.** 3, 1, 2
- **D.** 3, 2, 1

1.MD.A.1

4. Which fish is the longest?

Answer: _____

1.MD.A.1

5. Put the ribbons in order from the longest to the shortest.

- **A.** 1, 2, 3
- **B.** 3, 2, 1
- **C.** 3, 1, 2
- **D.** 2, 1, 3

1.MD.A.1

TIP of the DAY

We can always compare the length of an object with one or more objects.

1. Put the vegetables in order from the longest to the shortest.

   A. cucumber, potato, carrot
   B. cucumber, carrot, potato
   C. potato, carrot, cucumber
   D. carrot, cucumber, potato

1.MD.A.1

2. Put the animals in order from the shortest to the longest.

   A. pig, goat, horse
   B. goat, horse, pig
   C. goat, pig, horse
   D. pig, horse, goat

1.MD.A.1

3. Which insect is shorter?

   Beetle   Dragonfly

   Answer: _____

1.MD.A.1

4. Put the ships in order from the longest to the shortest.

   A. 1, 2, 3
   B. 2, 3, 1
   C. 1, 3, 2
   D. 3, 2, 1

1.MD.A.1

5. Put the objects in order from the shortest to the longest.

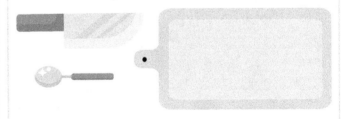

   A. Spoon, knife, cutting board
   B. cutting board, knife, spoon
   C. knife, spoon, cutting board
   D. knife, cutting board, spoon

1.MD.A.1

TIP
of the
DAY

We should already have an idea on how to compare objects that we are familiar with.
Which of the following is longer in length?
          A) Ladybug
          B) Paperclip

1. Put the objects in order from the longest to the shortest.

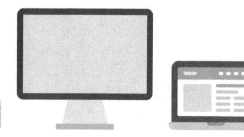

- **A.** laptop, camera, TV
- **B.** TV, laptop, camera
- **C.** camera, TV, laptop
- **D.** TV, camera, laptop

1.MD.A.1

2. Put the birds in order from the shortest to the longest.

- **A.** 2, 3, 1
- **B.** 3, 2, 1
- **C.** 2, 1, 3
- **D.** 1, 3, 2

1.MD.A.1

3. Which animal is longer?

Crocodile   Lizard

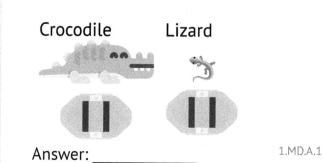

Answer: _____

1.MD.A.1

4. Put the objects in order from the longest to the shortest

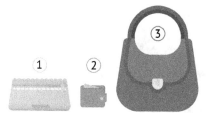

- **A.** 2, 1, 3
- **B.** 2, 3, 1
- **C.** 1, 3, 2
- **D.** 3, 1, 2

1.MD.A.1

5. Which fish is longer?

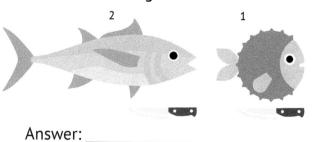

Answer: _____

1.MD.A.1

TIP of the DAY

We should already have an idea of how to compare objects that we are familiar with.
Which of the following is longer in length?
  A) Table
  B) Pencil

1. Put the fruits in order from the shortest to the longest.

   A. Banana, plum, orange
   B. Plum, orange, banana
   C. Orange, banana, plum
   D. Banana, orange, plum

   1.MD.A.1

2. Which shoe is shorter?

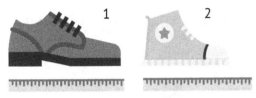

   Answer: _____

   1.MD.A.1

3. Put the objects in order from the longest to the shortest.

   A. marker, eraser, glue
   B. eraser, glue, marker
   C. marker, glue, eraser
   D. glue, eraser, marker

   1.MD.A.1

4. Put the cars in order from the shortest to the longest.

   A. 1, 3, 2
   B. 1, 2, 3
   C. 2, 1, 3
   D. 3, 1, 2

   1.MD.A.1

5. Put the objects in order from the longest to the shortest.

   A. scissors, hammer, saw
   B. hammer, saw, scissors
   C. saw, scissors, hammer
   D. saw, hammer, scissors

   1.MD.A.1

TIP *of the* **DAY**

We should already have an idea on how to compare objects that we are familiar with.
Which of the following is longer in length?
        A) Pen
        B) Car

WEEK 15 : DAY 5

1. Put the caterpillars in order from the shortest to the longest.

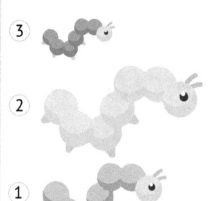

A. 1, 2, 3
B. 2, 1, 3
C. 3, 1, 2
D. 3, 2, 1

1.MD.A.1

2. Which rectangle is the shortest?

A. 1
B. 2
C. 3
D. Same length

1.MD.A.1

3. Put the pieces of furniture in order from the longest to the shortest.

A. chair, table, sofa
B. table, chair, sofa
C. sofa, chair, table
D. sofa, table, chair

1.MD.A.1

4. Which animal is the longest in length?

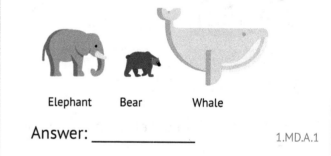

Elephant   Bear   Whale

Answer: _____

1.MD.A.1

5. Which bakery product is the longest?

Answer: _____

1.MD.A.1

DAY 6
Challenge question

Which line is longer? The left or the right? _____

1.MD.A.1

100

ARGOPREP.COM

VIDEO
EXPLANATIONS

In Week 16, we will understand the length of an object by using smaller objects.

You can find detailed video explanations of each problem in the book by visiting:
ArgoPrep.com

WEEK 16 : DAY 1

1. How long is the crocodile?

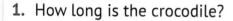

A. 6 stars
B. 7 stars
C. 8 stars
D. 9 stars

1.MD.A.2

2. How long is the fish?

A. 6 snowflakes
B. 7 snowflakes
C. 8 snowflakes
D. 9 snowflakes

1.MD.A.2

3. How many flowers long is the hot dog?

Answer: _____ flowers.   1.MD.A.2

4. How long is the car?

A. 9 coins   C. 7 coins
B. 8 coins   D. 6 coins   1.MD.A.2

5. How long is the album?

A. 1 marker   C. 3 markers
B. 2 markers   D. 4 markers   1.MD.A.2

6. How many beetles long is the hedgehog?

Answer: _____ beetles.   1.MD.A.2

TIP of the DAY

When doing different kinds of problems, take time to remember the same kinds of problems that you did before.

1. How long is the house?

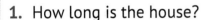

A. 2 bills
B. 3 bills
C. 4 bills
D. 5 bills

1.MD.A.2

2. How long is the candy bar?

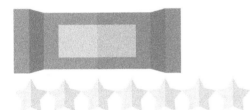

A. 5 stars
B. 6 stars
C. 7 stars
D. 8 stars

1.MD.A.2

3. How many seashells long is the crab?

Answer: _____ seashells

1.MD.A.2

4. How long is the cucumber?

A. 3 snowflakes
B. 4 snowflakes
C. 5 snowflakes
D. 6 snowflakes

1.MD.A.2

5. How many bricks long is the plane?

Answer: _____ bricks

1.MD.A.2

TIP of the DAY

If we know the length of one thing, we can use it to measure other things.

1. How long is the dragon?

A. 3 snowflakes
B. 4 snowflakes
C. 5 snowflakes
D. 6 snowflakes

1.MD.A.2

2. How long is the submarine?

A. 3 bills
B. 4 bills
C. 5 bills
D. 6 bills

1.MD.A.2

3. How many candies long is the bike?

Answer: _____ candies.

1.MD.A.2

4. How long is the cake?

A. 9 coins   C. 7 coins
B. 8 coins   D. 6 coins

1.MD.A.2

5. How many flowers long is the sofa?

Answer: _____ flowers.

1.MD.A.2

TIP of the DAY

The length is how long something is. We can put lengths together to find the total length.

1. How long are the scissors?

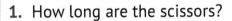

A. 6 snowflakes
B. 7 snowflakes
C. 8 snowflakes
D. 9 snowflakes

1.MD.A.2

2. How long is the ship?

A. 6 seashells   C. 8 seashells
B. 7 seashells   D. 9 seashells

1.MD.A.2

3. How many bricks long is the helicopter?

Answer: _____ bricks.   1.MD.A.2

4. How long is the dinosaur?

A. 7 leaves
B. 8 leaves
C. 9 leaves
D. 10 leaves

1.MD.A.2

5. How long is the airship?

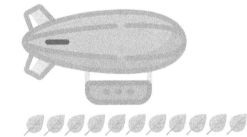

A. 8 leaves
B. 7 leaves
C. 6 leaves
D. 5 leaves

1.MD.A.2

TIP
of the
DAY

Here's a fun activity for you to try. Take an eraser and a notebook. How many erasers long is the notebook?

WEEK 16 : DAY 5

1. How long is the candy?

A. 6 snowflakes
B. 7 snowflakes
C. 9 snowflakes
D. 10 snowflakes

1.MD.A.2

2. How long is the camel?

A. 7 beetles
B. 8 beetles
C. 9 beetles
D. 10 beetles

1.MD.A.2

3. How many paper clips long is the laptop?

Answer: _____ paper clips.

1.MD.A.2

4. How long is the flower?

A. 4 leaves
B. 5 leaves
C. 6 leaves
D. 7 leaves

1.MD.A.2

5. How many bills long is the wagon?

Answer: _____ bills.

1.MD.A.2

DAY 6
Challenge question

How many leaves long are the dog and the fox?

_____

1.MD.A.2

WEEK 17

ARGOPREP.COM

VIDEO
EXPLANATIONS

What time is it? In Week 17, we will learn and write about time.

You can find detailed video explanations of each problem in the book by visiting:
ArgoPrep.com

1. Which clock shows 7:00?

1   2   3   4

A. 1   **C.** 3

B. 2   **D.** 4

1.MD.B.3

2. What time does the clock show?

A. 3:00   **C.** 4:00

B. 3:30   **D.** 4:30

1.MD.B.3

3. Which clock shows half past 2?

   2:30

1   2   3   4

A. 1

B. 2

C. 3

D. 4

1.MD.B.3

4. Write in words what time the clock shows.

Answer: _____

1.MD.B.3

5. Which clocks show the same time?

1   2   3   4

A. 1 and 2

B. 2 and 3

C. 3 and 4

D. 4 and 1

1.MD.B.3

6. What time does the clock show?

Answer: _____

1.MD.B.3

1. Which clock shows 4:30?

1   2   3   4

A. 1   **C.** 3

B. 2   **D.** 4

1.MD.B.3

2. Which clock shows eight o'clock?

1   2   3   4

A. 1   **C.** 3

B. 2   **D.** 4

1.MD.B.3

3. What time does the clock show?

Answer: _____

1.MD.B.3

4. Which clock shows half past 5?

1   2   3   4

A. 1   **C.** 3

B. 2   **D.** 4

1.MD.B.3

5. Which clocks show the same time?

1   2   3   4

A. 1 and 2   **C.** 2 and 3

B. 1 and 3   **D.** 2 and 4

1.MD.B.3

6. Which clock shows half past 6?

1   2   3   4

A. 1   **C.** 3

B. 2   **D.** 4

1.MD.B.3

TIP
of the
DAY

When reading a pictograph, be sure to check the key to see what one picture is equal to.

1. Which clocks show the same time?

A. 3 and 2   C. 2 and 1

B. 4 and 1   D. 3 and 4

1.MD.B.3

2. What time does the clock show?

Answer: _____

1.MD.B.3

3. Which clock shows 5:30?

A. 3   C. 4

B. 1   D. 2

1.MD.B.3

4. Which clocks show three o'clock?

A. 3 and 2   C. 2 and 1

B. 4 and 1   D. 3 and 4

1.MD.B.3

5. What time does the clock show?

Answer: _____

1.MD.B.3

6. Which clocks show the same time?

A. 1 and 2   C. 2 and 1

B. 4 and 1   D. 3 and 4

1.MD.B.3

TIP of the DAY

Another way to tell time is to tell the minutes after the hour that has just passed and the number of minutes to the next hour.

3:15 is also 15 minutes after 3

WEEK 17 : DAY 4

---

1. Which clock shows 2:30?

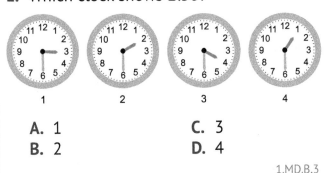

1   2   3   4

A. 1   C. 3
B. 2   D. 4

1.MD.B.3

---

4. Which clocks show the same time?

1   2   3   4

A. 1 and 2   C. 2 and 3
B. 1 and 3   D. 3 and 4

1.MD.B.3

---

2. Which clock shows half past 9?

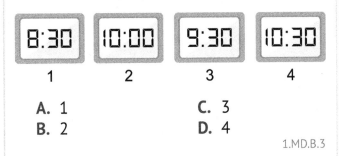

1   2   3   4

A. 1   C. 3
B. 2   D. 4

1.MD.B.3

---

5. What time does the clock show?

A. 6:30   C. 9:30
B. 5:30   D. 8:30

1.MD.B.3

---

3. What time does the clock show?

Answer: _____

1.MD.B.3

---

6. Write in words what time the clock shows.

6:30

Answer: _____

1.MD.B.3

TIP of the DAY

The times are repeated 2 times each day. The a.m. times are for the first part of the day (from 12:00 midnight until 12:00 noon). The p.m. times are for the second part of the day (from 12:00 noon until 12:00 midnight).

1. Which clock shows 10:00?

A. 1   C. 3
B. 2   D. 4

1.MD.B.3

2. Which clocks show the same time?

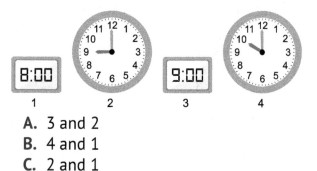

A. 3 and 2
B. 4 and 1
C. 2 and 1
D. 3 and 4

1.MD.B.3

3. What time does the clock show?

Answer: _____

1.MD.B.3

4. Which clocks show the same time?

A. 1 and 2   C. 1 and 4
B. 2 and 3   D. 2 and 4

1.MD.B.3

5. Which clock shows half past 1?

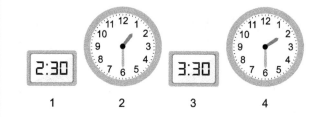

A. 1   C. 3
B. 2   D. 4

1.MD.B.3

6. What time does the clock show?

Answer: _____

1.MD.B.3

DAY 6
Challenge qvestion

Which clocks show the same time?

_____

1.MD.B.3

112

WEEK 18

VIDEO EXPLANATIONS ▶ ARGOPREP.COM

Week 18 is all about representing and interpreting data.

You can find detailed video explanations of each problem in the book by visiting:
ArgoPrep.com

Mrs. Sanders has roses, tulips and chamomiles in her garden. The number of flowers are in the chart below. Use the chart to answer questions 1 through 3.

	Roses	Tulips	Chamomiles
7			
6		▓	
5		▓	
4	▓	▓	
3	▓	▓	
2	▓	▓	
1	▓	▓	

The graph below shows students who enjoy going to the park, movies or on a roller coaster.

	park	movies	roller coaster
9			
8			
7			
6			
5	▓		
4	▓		
3	▓	▓	
2	▓	▓	
1	▓	▓	

1. How many flowers does Mrs. Sanders have in total?

   A. 12   C. 14
   B. 13   D. 15   1.MD.C.4

2. How many more chamomile than roses?

   A. 1   C. 3
   B. 2   D. 4   1.MD.C.4

3. Which flower is the most popular in Mrs. Sanders' garden?

   A. rose   C. chamomile
   B. tulip   1.MD.C.4

4. Which activity do students most enjoy according to this graph?

   A. park   C. roller coaster
   B. movies
                              1.MD.C.4

5. How many students in total are represented in this graph above?

   A. 13   C. 15
   B. 14   D. 16   1.MD.C.4

6. How many more students chose roller coaster than the movies?

   A. 1   C. 3
   B. 2   D. 4   1.MD.C.4

TIP
of the
DAY

It is very important you know how to understand data when it is presented on a chart or table.

At the café the visitors bought Coke, tea and coffee. Use the chart to answer questions 1 through 3.

Chosen drinks			
9			
8			
7			
6			
5			
4			
3			
2			
1			
	Coke	Tea	Coffee

Kids either chose a red, yellow or green balloon to have at the party. Use the chart to answer questions 4 through 6.

9			
8			
7			
6			
5			
4			
3			
2			
1			
	red balloons	yellow balloons	green balloons

1. How many visitors were at the café?

A. 16   C. 18
B. 17   D. 19

1.MD.C.4

4. How many balloons were there in total according to the chart?

A. 15   C. 17
B. 16   D. 18

1.MD.C.4

2. Which drink was the least popular?

A. Coke   C. Coffee
B. Tea

1.MD.C.4

5. Which color balloon was the most selected by kids?

A. red   C. blue
B. yellow

1.MD.C.4

3. How many more visitors chose Coke than Tea?

A. 1   C. 3
B. 2   D. 4

1.MD.C.4

6. How many more yellow balloons than green ones were chosen by kids?

A. 2   C. 4
B. 3   D. 5

1.MD.C.4

TIP of the DAY

When looking at a bar graph, pay attention to the values that the graph indicates. This will help you to figure out the values that the bars represent.

Ms. Smith has a certain number of cats, dogs and rabbits that are represented in the chart. Use the chart below to answer questions 1 through 3.

9			
8			
7			
6			
5			
4			
3			
2			
1			
	🐱	🐶	🐰

The chart below represents different color uniforms worn by students attending gym class.

	Selection of sports uniform		
10			
9			
8			
7			
6			
5			
4			
3			
2			
1			
	blue	yellow	red

1. How many more cats than rabbits are there?

   A. 1   **C.** 3

   B. 2   **D.** 4   1.MD.C.4

2. How many more rabbits are there than dogs?

   A. 1   **C.** 3

   B. 2   **D.** 4   1.MD.C.4

3. What is the total number of pets shown in the chart?

   A. 16   **C.** 14

   B. 15   **D.** 13   1.MD.C.4

4. Which sports uniform is the most popular among the kids?

   A. blue   **C.** red

   B. yellow   1.MD.C.4

5. How many more kids chose the red sports uniform than the yellow one?

   A. 6   **C.** 4

   B. 5   **D.** 3   1.MD.C.4

6. How many color uniforms are represented here in total?

   A. 15   **C.** 19

   B. 18   **D.** 16   1.MD.C.4

TIP
of the
DAY

Graphs are a great way to understand a set or a group of data. Once you collect your data, turning it into a bar graph helps you to understand the information you collected.

A survey was conducted in a class to see how many students had a fish, bird or dog as a pet. The results are shown below.

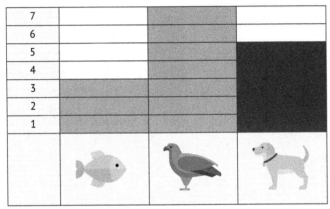

Steven watched the cars driving along the street through the window of his house. He decided to write down the amount of cars he saw passing by.

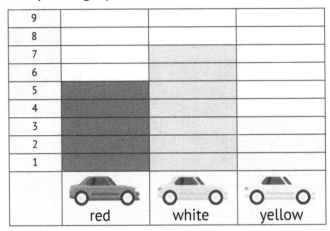

1. How many pets are there in total in the chart?

    A. 14
    B. 15
    C. 16
    D. 17

    1.MD.C.4

2. How many more students have a bird as a pet than a fish?

    A. 2
    B. 3
    C. 4
    D. 5

    1.MD.C.4

3. What color car did Steven record passing by the most?

    A. red
    B. white
    C. yellow

    1.MD.C.4

4. How many more white cars than red cars were recorded in the chart?

    A. 1
    B. 2
    C. 3
    D. 4

    1.MD.C.4

5. How many cars did Steven record in total?

    A. 12
    B. 13
    C. 14
    D. 15

    1.MD.C.4

TIP of the DAY

You can read a bar graph, but can you create one? When creating a bar graph, make sure to label everything! It's important to know what the graph is mostly about and what the bars represent.

ASSESSMENT

Students chose a hot dog, hamburger or pizza for lunch time. Using the chart, answer questions 1 through 3.

7			
6			
5			
4			
3			
2			
1			
	🌭	🍔	🍕

1. Which meal is the most popular?

   A. hot dog   **C.** pizza
   B. hamburger

1.MD.C.4

2. How many more students chose hot dog than pizza?

   A. 1   **C.** 3
   B. 2   **D.** 4

1.MD.C.4

3. What is the total number of students represented in the chart?

   A. 12   **C.** 14
   B. 13   **D.** 15

1.MD.C.4

Use the chart below to answer questions 4 to 6.

9			
8			
7			
6			
5			
4			
3			
2			
1			
	✏️	📓 book	🔪

4. How many more pencils are there than markers?

   A. 1   **C.** 3
   B. 2   **D.** 4

1.MD.C.4

5. How many more notebooks are there than markers?

   A. 1   **C.** 3
   B. 2   **D.** 4

1.MD.C.4

6. What is the total number of pencils, notebooks and markers shown on the chart above?

   A. 15   **C.** 17
   B. 16   **D.** 18

1.MD.C.4

DAY 6
Challenge qvestion

There are 5 red cars, 4 blue cars and 2 black cars in the parking lot. How many more red cars are there than black cars in the parking lot?

_____

1.MD.C.4

In Week 19, we learn about different shapes and their attributes.

You can find detailed video explanations of each problem in the book by visiting:
ArgoPrep.com

1. How many squares do you count?

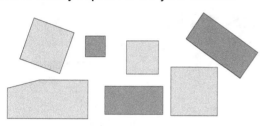

A. 2   **C.** 4
B. 3   **D.** 5   1.GA.1

2. Which shape is NOT a square?

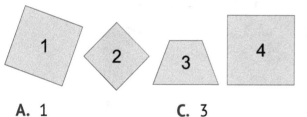

A. 1   **C.** 3
B. 2   **D.** 4   1.GA.1

3. Why is this shape NOT a hexagon?

A. It is gray.
B. Is does not have six angles.
C. The sides are touching.
D. It is big.   1.GA.1

4. How many sides does a trapezoid have?

A. 3
B. 4
C. 5
D. 6   1.GA.1

5. These shapes are triangles.

Why is this shape NOT a triangle?

A. It is another color.
B. It is smaller.
C. It is a square.
D. It has four angles.   1.GA.1

6. Which shape is a pentagon?

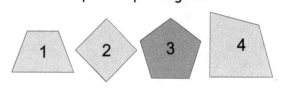

Answer: _____   1.GA.1

TIP of the DAY

Flat shapes have straight sides that we can count.

1. You're making a trapezoid. How many more lines do you need to draw?

A. 1
B. 2
C. 3
D. 4

1.GA.1

4. A rectangle always ...

A. has three sides
B. is bigger than other shapes
C. is smaller than other shapes
D. has four angles

1.GA.1

2. Which shape is a square?

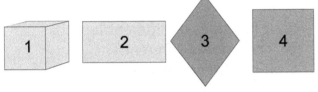

A. 1
B. 2
C. 3
D. 4

1.GA.1

5. Which shape is a hexagon?

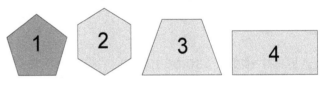

A. 1
B. 2
C. 3
D. 4

1.GA.1

3. How many pentagons do you count?

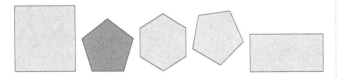

A. 1
B. 2
C. 3
D. 4

1.GA.1

6. A triangle can NEVER ...

A. have sides of different length.
B. be tilted.
C. have four sides.
D. be bigger than a trapezoid.

1.GA.1

TIP of the DAY

Shapes that are made of straight sides have angles where the sides bend. The number of angles are the same as the number of sides

1. How many triangles do you count?

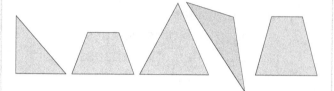

A. 1
B. 2
C. 3
D. 4

1.GA.1

2. What shape can be made of these lines?

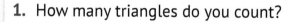

A. triangle
B. square
C. pentagon
D. rectangle

1.GA.1

3. What is the difference between a square and a trapezoid?

A. A square has fewer angles.
B. Squares are smaller than trapezoids.
C. A square is longer than a trapezoid.
D. A square has all equal sides.

1.GA.1

4. These shapes are squares.

Why is this shape NOT a square?

A. It has sides of different lengths.
B. The color is different.
C. It is different in size.
D. It is longer.

1.GA.1

5. How many sides does a hexagon have?

A. 3
B. 4
C. 5
D. 6

1.GA.1

6. A square can NEVER ...

A. have four sides.
B. have sides of different lengths.
C. have two sides that don't touch.
D. have four angles.

1.GA.1

TIP
of the
DAY

Be careful with questions that ask NOT.

1. How many triangles do you count?

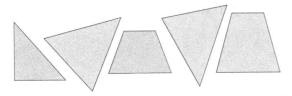

A. 1
B. 2
C. 3
D. 4

1.GA.1

2. How many triangles do you count?

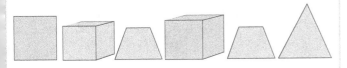

A. 1
B. 2
C. 3
D. 4

1.GA.1

3. A trapezoid can NEVER...

A. have sides of different lengths.
B. have four angles.
C. be bigger than a rectangle.
D. have sides of the same length.

1.GA.1

4. You're making a hexagon. How many more lines do you need to draw?

_____ _____

A. 2
B. 3
C. 4
D. 5

1.GA.1

5. How many sides does a rectangle have?

A. 3
B. 4
C. 5
D. 6

1.GA.1

6. What is the difference between a pentagon and a trapezoid?

A. A pentagon has five sides.
B. A pentagon is bigger than a trapezoid.
C. The sides in a pentagon do not touch.
D. A pentagon has angles.

1.GA.1

TIP
of the
DAY

Know the differences between a circle, triangle, square, rectangle and pentagon.

1. Which shape is NOT a triangle?

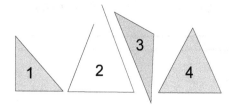

A. 1
B. 2
C. 3
D. 4

1.GA.1

2. These shapes are all rectangles.

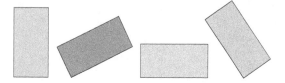

Why is this shape NOT a rectangle?

A. It has four sides.
B. It has all equal sides.
C. It has no angles.
D. It has three sides.

1.GA.1

3. How many more angles does a pentagon have than a triangle?

A. 1
B. 2
C. 3
D. 4

1.GA.1

4. What do these shapes have in common?

A. They are of the same size.
B. They have equal sides.
C. They are of the same color.
D. They have four angles.

1.GA.1

5. A pentagon can NEVER...

A. have six angles.
B. have equal sides.
C. be smaller than a square.
D. be bigger than a square.

1.GA.1

DAY 6
Challenge qvestion

A book has what geometric shape?

_____

1.GA.1

124

WEEK 20

VIDEO EXPLANATIONS ▶ ARGOPREP.COM

Woah! Congratulations on making it this far. In Week 20, we will learn about two-dimensional shapes, three-dimensional shapes and how to partition circles and rectangles into two or four equal parts.

You can find detailed video explanations of each problem in the book by visiting:
ArgoPrep.com

1. This shape is made of...

- **A.** One square and one trapezoid
- **B.** One square and one triangle
- **C.** Two squares
- **D.** Three triangles

1.GA.2 & 1.GA.3

2. You can push together two trapezoids to make...

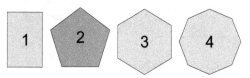

- **A.** 1
- **B.** 2
- **C.** 3
- **D.** 4

1.GA.2 & 1.GA.3

3. This shape is made of ...

- **A.** Two triangles
- **B.** Three triangles
- **C.** Four triangles
- **D.** One triangle and one square

1.GA.2 & 1.GA.3

4. You can push together two triangles to make...

- **A.** A square
- **C.** A rectangle
- **B.** A trapezoid
- **D.** A triangle

1.GA.2 & 1.GA.3

5. You want to make this cylinder. You can make the cylinder with ...

- **A.** One circle and one rectangle
- **B.** One circle and one triangle
- **C.** One circle and two rectangles
- **D.** Two circles and one rectangle

1.GA.2 & 1.GA.3

6. Which shape could be made of three triangles?

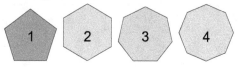

- **A.** 1
- **C.** 3
- **B.** 2
- **D.** 4

1.GA.2 & 1.GA.3

TIP *of the* DAY

Rectangles and squares are both made with 4 straight lines.

126

1. You can push together two triangles to make...

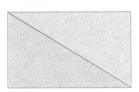

- **A.** A triangle
- **B.** A rectangle
- **C.** A pentagon
- **D.** A trapezoid

1.GA.2 & 1.GA.3

2. Harry is using six squares of cardboard to make a three-dimensional shape. What shape does Harry want to make?

- **A.** A hexagon
- **B.** A cylinder
- **C.** A cone
- **D.** A cube

1.GA.2 & 1.GA.3

3. A trapezoid could be made of...

- **A.** two rectangles
- **B.** one rectangle and one triangle
- **C.** one triangle and two rectangles
- **D.** one rectangle and two triangles

1.GA.2 & 1.GA.3

4. What shapes do you need to use to make a cone?

- **A.** 1 and 2
- **B.** 2 and 3
- **C.** 3 and 4
- **D.** 4 and 1

1.GA.2 & 1.GA.3

5. A star could be made of ...

- **A.** One pentagon and five triangles
- **B.** One quadrangle and five triangles
- **C.** Six triangles
- **D.** Two squares and five triangles

1.GA.2 & 1.GA.3

6. What shape is a half-circle?

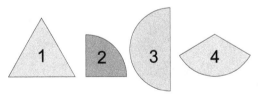

- **A.** 1
- **B.** 2
- **C.** 3
- **D.** 4

1.GA.2 & 1.GA.3

TIP of the DAY

Rectangles have two sets of equal sides with equal lengths, while all sides of a square are equal in length.

1. Which shape is divided into halves?

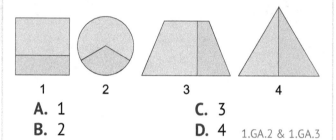

A. 1   C. 3
B. 2   D. 4   1.GA.2 & 1.GA.3

2. This shape is made of...

A. Two triangles and one rectangle
B. Two triangles and three rectangles
C. One triangle and one rectangle
D. One triangle and three rectangles

1.GA.2 & 1.GA.3

3. Which shape is divided into quarters?

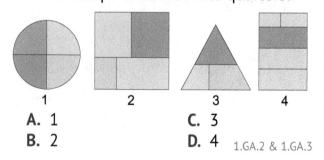

A. 1   C. 3
B. 2   D. 4   1.GA.2 & 1.GA.3

4. How many squares of paper are used to make a shape shown in the picture?

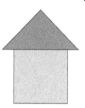

A. Two squares
B. One square and a half-square
C. One square and a quarter-square
D. three squares

1.GA.2 & 1.GA.3

5. Which shape is a quarter-circle?

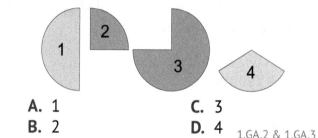

A. 1   C. 3
B. 2   D. 4   1.GA.2 & 1.GA.3

6. Which shape is NOT divided into quarters?

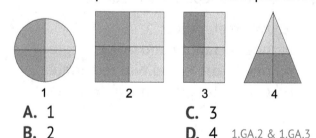

A. 1   C. 3
B. 2   D. 4   1.GA.2 & 1.GA.3

TIP *of the* **DAY**   *A triangle always has 3 sides.*

1. Which rectangle is divided into quarters?

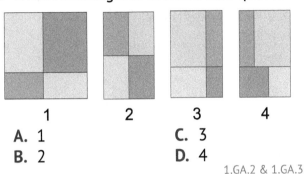

1   2   3   4

A. 1

B. 2

C. 3

D. 4

1.GA.2 & 1.GA.3

2. This shape is made of ...

A. One triangle and one rectangle

B. One triangle and one square

C. One triangle, one rectangle and two circles

D. One cylinder and one cone

1.GA.2 & 1.GA.3

3. Mia ordered half a pizza and Chloé ordered two fourths of a pizza. Who ate more?

Answer: _____

1.GA.2 & 1.GA.3

4. How many such shapes do you need to make a circle?

A. 2

B. 3

C. 4

D. 6

1.GA.2 & 1.GA.3

5. If the square is divided as shown in the picture, how many quarters do we get?

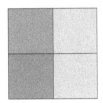

Answer: _____

1.GA.2 & 1.GA.3

5. Matthew gave half a pie to Vicky. How many parts did Matthew divide the pie into?

Answer: _____

1.GA.2 & 1.GA.3

TIP of the DAY

A shape has to be divided into equal parts to be able to assign a unit fraction. If a shape has four parts, and they are equal in size, each of them would be called 1/4.

WEEK 20 : DAY 5

1. Which shape is NOT divided into quarters?

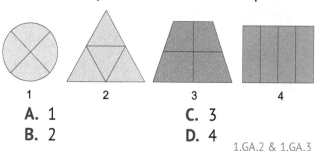

A. 1   C. 3
B. 2   D. 4

1.GA.2 & 1.GA.3

2. How many fourths of a square are in the picture?

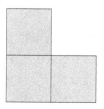

Answer: _____

1.GA.2 & 1.GA.3

3. Logan wants to make a quarter-sheet drawing. How does Logan have to place the picture on a sheet?

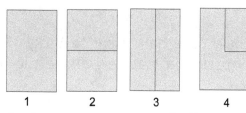

A. 1   C. 3
B. 2   D. 4   1.GA.2 & 1.GA.3

4. Look at the picture below. Which cylinder equals the quarter of the biggest cylinder?

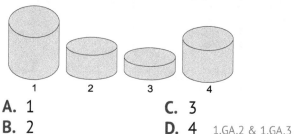

A. 1   C. 3
B. 2   D. 4   1.GA.2 & 1.GA.3

5. How many quarters is the shape A smaller than shape B?

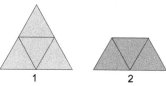

A. One quarter
B. Two quarters
C. Three quarters
D. Four quarters   1.GA.2 & 1.GA.3

6. In the picture you can see a part of a circle. How many quarters do you need to make a whole circle?

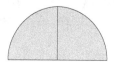

A. 1   C. 3
B. 2   D. 4   1.GA.2 & 1.GA.3

DAY 6
Challenge qvestion

What is bigger: two halves or three fourths?

_____

1.GA.2 & 1.GA.3

THE
END

**Great job finishing all 20 weeks!
You should be ready for any test.**

VIDEO
EXPLANATIONS

ARGOPREP.COM

Try this assessment to see how much you've learned - good luck!

4. Eight children were playing at the playground. More children came to play at the playground. There are 15 children at the playground now. How many children came?

$$8 + \boxed{} = 15$$

A. 5
B. 6
C. 7
D. 8

5. Oliver had 14 pencils. He gave some pencils to his sister. Now Oliver has 8 pencils. How many pencils did Oliver give to his sister?

$$14 - \boxed{} = 8$$

A. 5
B. 6
C. 7
D. 8

6. Elizabeth had 16 books. She gave away 9 books to the library. How many books does Elizabeth now own?

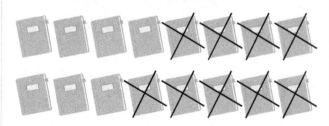

Answer: _____

7. William has 6 toy ships, Gabe has 7 toy ships and Nolan has only 3 toy ships. How many toy ships do the friends have in all?

$$6 + 7 + 3 = \boxed{}$$

A. 14
B. 15
C. 16
D. 17

8. There are green, yellow and white marbles in a bag. The bag has a total of 18 marbles. If there are 9 green marbles and 5 yellow marbles, how many white marbles are in the bag?

$$9 + 5 + \boxed{} = 18$$

A. 4   C. 6
B. 5   D. 7

9. Hannah, Charlotte and Patty drew a total of 20 pictures. Hannah drew 6 pictures, Charlotte drew 7 pictures. How many pictures did Patty draw?

$$6 + 7 + \boxed{} = 20$$

A. 4
B. 5
C. 6
D. 7

ASSESSMENT

10. Which of the following number sentences is the same as $4 + 15 = 19$?

    A. $4 + 5 = 9$
    B. $5 + 15 = 20$
    C. $14 + 4 = 18$
    D. $15 + 4 = 19$

11. Fill in the blank:

$$12 + 5 = 11 + \boxed{} + 2$$

    A. 3
    B. 4
    C. 5
    D. 6

12. $8 + 6 + 3 = 17$. What is $6 + 3 + 8$?

    A. 14
    B. 15
    C. 16
    D. 17

13. Which number can complete BOTH number sentences?

$$6 + 8 = \boxed{} \qquad \boxed{} - 8 = 6$$

    A. 12
    B. 13
    C. 14
    D. 15

14. Paul needs to bake 15 cakes. He has already baked 8 cakes. Which number sentence shows how many more cakes Paul needs to bake?

    A. $15 - 8 = \boxed{}$
    B. $15 + 8 = \boxed{}$
    C. $\boxed{} - 15 = 8$
    D. $15 - \boxed{} = 8$

15. Which number can complete BOTH number sentences?

$$\boxed{} + 4 = 15 \qquad 15 - 4 = \boxed{}$$

Answer: _____

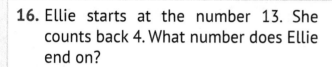
16. Ellie starts at the number 13. She counts back 4. What number does Ellie end on?

A. 11
B. 10
C. 9
D. 8

17. Abigail had 12 flowers. She picked up 6 more. Then Abigail gifted 7 flowers to her mother. How many flowers does Abigail have now?

A. 11
B. 12
C. 13
D. 14

18. Matthew had 14 toys. Then 5 toys more were gifted to him. Which number sentence shows how many toys Matthew has now?

A. 14 - 5 = 9
B. 5 + 9 = 14
C. 14 + 5 = 19
D. 19 - 5 = 14

19. 12 + 7 = 10 + 2 + 7 =

A. 16
B. 17
C. 18
D. 19

20. 16 - 12 = 16 - 10 - 2 =

A. 3
B. 4
C. 5
D. 6

21. Sam has 7 red markers. Bill has 8 markers (3 blue and 5 yellow). How many markers do Sam and Bill have in all?

Answer: _____

22. There is an equal amount of people in house A and house B. There are 5 people in house A. How many people are there in house B?

Answer: _____

23. Which number sentence is true?

A. 12 + 7 = 18
B. 15 - 4 = 12
C. 9 + 8 = 17
D. 14 - 7 = 6

24. Which number sentence is FALSE?

A. 5 + 7 = 11
B. 8 + 6 = 14
C. 12 - 7 = 5
D. 14 + 2 = 16

25. ▲ is a mystery number. ▲ + 14 = 17? What is ▲ ?

A. 1
B. 2
C. 3
D. 4

26. A total of 15 balls can fit into a basket. If there are 9 balls in the basket already, how many more balls can fit in the basket?

A. 5
B. 6
C. 7
D. 8

27. What is the missing number:

$$18 - \boxed{} = 9$$

A. 10
B. 8
C. 11
D. 9

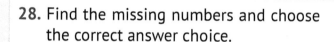

28. Find the missing numbers and choose the correct answer choice.

1	2	3		5	6	7	8	9	10
11	12	13	14	15	16	17	18	19	20
21	22	23	24	25		27	28	29	30
31	32	33	34	35	36	37	38	39	40
41	42	43	44	45	46	47	48	49	50
51	52	53	54	55	56	57	58	59	60
61	62	63	64	65	66	67	68	69	70
71	72	73	74	75	76	77	78	79	80
81	82	83	84	75	86	87	88	89	90
91	92		94	95	96	97	98	99	100
101	102	103	104	105	106	107	108	109	110
111	112	113	114	115	116		118	119	120

A. 4, 32, 94, 105   **C.** 4, 26, 94, 107

B. 4, 26, 93, 117   **D.** 4, 28, 86, 117

29. How many flowers do you see in the picture?

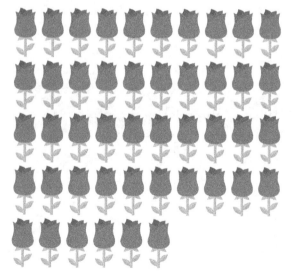

A. 44   **C.** 46

B. 45   **D.** 47

30. How do you write the number 76 in words?

   A. Seven and six

   B. Seventeen and six

   C. Sixty-seven

   D. Seventy-six

31. Count the baseballs. Select the correct answer choice.

   A. 54   **C.** 58

   B. 56   **D.** 60

32. Regroup the following expression. Note: Write a number from 0 to 9 in each box.

5 tens + 18 ones = ☐ tens + ☐ ones

   A. 5 and 8

   B. 8 and 5

   C. 6 and 8

   D. 6 and 7

33. Which answer choice below represents the number 73?

    A. 7 tens + 3 tens
    B. 70 tens + 3 ones
    C. 73 tens
    D. 7 tens + 3 ones

34. Look at the number sequences below and choose from greatest to least.

    A. 86, 75, 77, 23
    B. 65, 37, 21, 18
    C. 37, 65, 89, 77
    D. 78, 65, 54, 56

35. Which words make this statement true?

$$45 \underline{\hspace{2cm}} 54$$

    A. Is greater than
    B. Is less than
    C. Is equal to
    D. Is greater than or equal to

36. There are 15 students in group A. There are 15 students in group B. There are 19 students in group C. Choose the correct statement below.

    A. A group = B group = C group
    B. A group > B group = C group
    C. A group < B group < C group
    D. A group = B group < C group

37. Write the addition sentence that the model below shows.

$$\underline{\hspace{1.5cm}} + \underline{\hspace{1.5cm}} = \underline{\hspace{1.5cm}}$$

38. Which of the following is equal to 67 + 23? Choose the correct answer choice.

    A. 70
    B. 80
    C. 90
    D. 100

39. There were 22 passengers in one bus. There were 17 passengers in another bus. How many passengers were there in both buses?

    A. 2 tens + 2 ones + 17 tens = 37 ones
    B. 22 tens + 1 tens + 7 ones = 37 ones
    C. 2 tens + 2 tens + 1 tens + 7 ones = 47 ones
    D. 2 tens + 2 ones + 1 tens + 7 ones = 39 ones

ASSESSMENT

40. What number is 10 less than 65?

    A. 55
    B. 45
    C. 35
    D. 25

41. Using mental math, find the numbers that are 10 less and 10 more that the number shown below.

    _____ , 48 , _____

42. Mark collected 34 postcards and Claire collected ten postcards more. How many postcards did Claire collect?

    A. 24
    B. 44
    C. 54
    D. 64

43. Which number sentence matches the picture?

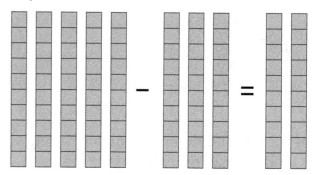

    A. 5 - 3 = 2
    B. 50 - 3 = 20
    C. 5 - 30 = 20
    D. 50 - 30 = 20

44. What is 80 - 40?

    A. 40
    B. 50
    C. 60
    D. 70

45. Which number sentence equals 90 - 30?

    A. 50 + 10
    B. 40 + 50
    C. 30 + 40
    D. 30 + 20

46. Put the animals in order from the shortest to the longest.

   A. Rhino, dog, zebra
   B. Rhino, zebra, dog
   C. Zebra, dog, rhino
   D. dog, zebra, rhino

47. What is longer?

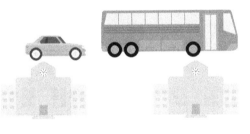

   Answer: _____

48. Put the stationery in order from the longest to the shortest.

   A. A pencil, a notebook, a ruler
   B. A ruler, a notebook, a pencil
   C. A notebook, a pencil, a ruler
   D. A notebook, a ruler, a pencil

49. How many tires long is the motorbike?

   A. 6   **C.** 8
   B. 7   **D.** 9

50. How many buttons long is the pant?

   Answer: _____

51. How many stars long is the ladder?

   A. 6   **C.** 10
   B. 8   **D.** 12

ASSESSMENT

52. What time does the clock show?

A. 6:00   **C.** 7:00
B. 6:30   **D.** 7:30

53. Which clocks show the same time?

1   2   3   4

A. 1 and 4
B. 2 and 3
C. 3 and 1
D. 4 and 2

54. Which clock shows 9:30?

1   2   3   4

A. 1
B. 2
C. 3
D. 4

Green, blue and red leaves were used to make a wreath. Use the charts to answer questions 52 through 54.

	green	blue	red
8			
7	■		
6	■		■
5	■	■	■
4	■	■	■
3	■	■	■
2	■	■	■
1	■	■	■

55. What color leaves was used the most?

     A. green
     B. blue
     C. red

56. How many more green leaves were used than blue leaves?

     A. 1
     B. 2
     C. 3
     D. 4

57. How many leaves were used in all?

     A. 15
     B. 16
     C. 17
     D. 18

58. These shapes are squares.

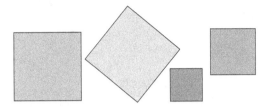

Why is this shape NOT a square?

A. The sides are not all equal.
B. The shape's size is different.
C. Not all its sides touch each other.
D. It has a different color.

59. You're making a hexagon. How many more lines do you need to draw?

A. 2   C. 4
B. 3   D. 5

60. How many rectangles do you count?

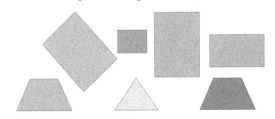

A. 2   C. 4
B. 3   D. 5

61. This shape is made of...

A. One rectangle and one cylinder
B. Three squares and one cylinder
C. One prism, one cylinder and one circle
D. One prism and one cylinder

62. Which shape is NOT divided into quarters?

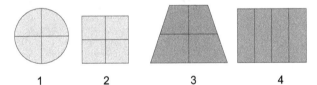

1   2   3   4

A. 1
B. 2
C. 3
D. 4

63. Wyatt had an apple pie and Audrey had a cherry pie. Both pies are the same size. Wyatt gave a half of his apple pie to Audrey. Audrey gave 2 quarters of her cherry pie to Wyatt.

Who has more now? _____

ANSWER KEY

VIDEO
EXPLANATIONS

ARGOPREP.COM

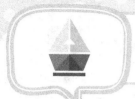

ANSWER KEY

WEEK 1

DAY 1	DAY 2	DAY 3	DAY 4	DAY 5
1. B	1. B	1. D	1. 7	1. 9
2. C	2. 14	2. 12	2. A	2. B
3. C	3. B	3. B	3. 7	3. C
4. D	4. A	4. B	4. 16	4. 6
5. B	5. 20	5. 4	5. C	5. C
6. B	6. 8	6. 8	6. 10	

WEEK 2

DAY 1	DAY 2	DAY 3	DAY 4	DAY 5
1. 10	1. C	1. B	1. B	1. C
2. C	2. C	2. C	2. 16	2. D
3. B	3. B	3. 15	3. 9	3. B
4. D	4. C	4. D	4. B	4. B
5. 19	5. A	5. D	5. A	5. B
6. B	6. D	6. 12	6. C	6. C

WEEK 3

DAY 1	DAY 2	DAY 3	DAY 4	DAY 5
1. C	1. D	1. C	1. C	1. C
2. D	2. C	2. C	2. C	2. A
3. B	3. 27	3. 23	3. 85	3. A
4. 90	4. B	4. D	4. D	4. 33
5. D	5. A	5. C	5. C	5. 99
6. C	6. D	6. C	6. B	6. D

WEEK 4

DAY 1	DAY 2	DAY 3	DAY 4	DAY 5
1. C	1. B	1. 20	1. B	1. C
2. A	2. 42	2. B	2. D	2. B
3. 2	3. C	3. 18	3. C	3. B
4. D	4. C	4. 66	4. C	4. C
5. C	5. C	5. C	5. B	5. 5
6. 24	6. 12	6. B		6. 71

WEEK 5

DAY 1	DAY 2	DAY 3	DAY 4	DAY 5
1. A	1. C	1. B	1. D	1. 5
2. B	2. C	2. 26	2. 25	2. 12
3. 21	3. A	3. 2	3. 46	3. C
4. 12	4. D	4. B	4. C	4. C
5. D	5. 22	5. A	5. 16	5. D
6. C	6. B	6. 6	6. 12	6. 22

WEEK 6

DAY 1	DAY 2	DAY 3	DAY 4	DAY 5
1. B	1. 6	1. D	1. 12	1. A
2. B	2. C	2. C	2. 7	2. B
3. D	3. 18	3. 20	3. B	3. 19
4. 19	4. 8	4. 6	4. B	4. 10
5. 5	5. 10	5. 9	5. C	5. D
6. 14	6. 8	6. 17	6. C	6. C

WEEK 7

DAY 1	DAY 2	DAY 3	DAY 4	DAY 5
1. D	1. C	1. B	1. 12	1. A
2. B	2. B	2. B	2. B	2. C
3. C	3. C	3. D	3. B	3. B
4. D	4. C	4. C	4. A	4. 12
5. 4	5. 8	5. 3	5. B	5. A
6. 14	6. D	6. C	6. D	6. C

WEEK 8

DAY 1	DAY 2	DAY 3	DAY 4	DAY 5
1. C	1. D	1. C	1. 6	1. B
2. B	2. B	2. 7	2. B	2. A
3. D	3. C	3. A	3. C	3. 4
4. B	4. 6	4. B	4. B	4. 7
5. 8	5. D	5. D	5. 9	5. B
6. B	6. B	6. 6	6. 5	6. D

ANSWER KEY

WEEK 9

DAY 1	DAY 2	DAY 3	DAY 4	DAY 5
1. B	1. C	1. 38	1. C	1. 10
2. B	2. B	2. C	2. B	2. C
3. B	3. C	3. B	3. 4,020	3. C
4. D	4. C	4. A	4. C	4. D
5. 44	5. B	5. B	5. B	5. D
				6. D

WEEK 10

DAY 1	DAY 2	DAY 3	DAY 4	DAY 5
1. 4 and 3	1. A	1. B	1. 7 and 2	1. B
2. B	2. 4 and 5	2. B	2. A	2. B
3. A	3. 4, 20, 0, 8	3. B	3. 30, 54,	3. A
4. B	4. 3 tens,	4. B	10, 15	4. A
5. 8	2 ones, 32	5. A	4. A	5. 8 and 8
	clouds	6. B	5. B	
	5. A		6. B	

WEEK 11

DAY 1	DAY 2	DAY 3	DAY 4	DAY 5
1. C	1. D	1. Strawber-	1. C	1. A
2. B	2. C	ries	2. C	2. B
3. B	3. C	2. Answers	3. <, <	3. D
4. C	4. A	may vary	4. Answers	4. Answers
5. D	5. B	3. B	may vary	may vary
6. B	6. A	4. A	5. B	5. A
		5. B, C	6. B	6. A
		6. B		

WEEK 12

DAY 1	DAY 2	DAY 3	DAY 4	DAY 5
1. B	1. B	1. A, B, C	1. C	1. C
2. C	2. 30	2. A	2. C	2. 26 + 33
3. 26 + 13	3. C	3. A	3. A	= 59
= 39	4. A	4. A, B, D	4. D	3. 26 + 51
4. C	5. D	5. 3 and 1	5. C	= 77
5. 6 and 3		6. D	6. A	
6. B				

WEEK 13

DAY 1	DAY 2	DAY 3	DAY 4	DAY 5
1. B	1. C	1. C	1. B	1. B
2. B	2. C	2. B	2. D	2. 34, 54
3. 66, 86	3. 21, 41	3. 45	3. C	3. B
4. C	4. B	4. 63, 83	4. B	4. C
5. B	5. 60	5. B	5. B	
6. A	6. C	6. C		

WEEK 14

DAY 1	DAY 2	DAY 3	DAY 4	DAY 5
1. C	1. D	1. B	1. C	1. D
2. D	2. B	2. 60	2. 20	2. A
3. C	3. A	3. C	3. C	3. 10
4. C	4. B	4. A	4. B	4. C
5. B	5. D	5. D	5. C	5. 40
6. 40	6. 50	6. 40	6. A	6. C

WEEK 15

DAY 1	DAY 2	DAY 3	DAY 4	DAY 5
1. D	1. B	1. B	1. B	1. C
2. A	2. C	2. C	2. 2	2. C
3. C	3. beetle	3. crocodile	3. C	3. D
4. 1 a shark	4. D	4. D	4. A	4. whale
5. D	5. A	5. 2	5. D	5. 2

WEEK 16

DAY 1	DAY 2	DAY 3	DAY 4	DAY 5
1. D	1. B	1. D	1. C	1. D
2. B	2. A	2. B	2. B	2. C
3. 4	3. 7	3. 5	3. 7	3. 7
4. B	4. D	4. A	4. D	4. B
5. C	5. 5	5. 9	5. A	5. 7
6. 4				

ANSWER KEY

WEEK 17

DAY 1	DAY 2	DAY 3	DAY 4	DAY 5
1. C	1. D	1. D	1. B	1. D
2. B	2. B	2. 01:00 or one o'clok	2. C	2. A
3. D	3. 11:30 or half past 11	3. A	3. ten o'clock	3. 9:30 or half past 9
4. half past 7		4. D	4. C	4. D
5. B	4. A	5. 6:00 or six o'clok	5. D	5. B
6. 1:30 or half past 1	5. C	6. B	6. 6:30 or half past six	6. 6:30 or half past six
	6. B			

WEEK 18

DAY 1	DAY 2	DAY 3	DAY 4	DAY 5
1. D	1. C	1. A	1. B	1. A
2. A	2. B	2. B	2. C	2. A
3. B	3. D	3. C	3. B	3. C
4. C	4. B	4. C	4. B	4. D
5. B	5. B	5. B	5. D	5. C
6. C	6. B	6. C		6. B

WEEK 19

DAY 1	DAY 2	DAY 3	DAY 4	DAY 5
1. C	1. B	1. C	1. C	1. B
2. C	2. D	2. C	2. A	2. C
3. B	3. B	3. D	3. D	3. B
4. B	4. D	4. A	4. A	4. D
5. D	5. B	5. D	5. B	5. A
6. 3	6. C	6. B	6. A	

WEEK 20

DAY 1	DAY 2	DAY 3	DAY 4	DAY 5
1. B	1. B	1. D	1. B	1. C
2. C	2. D	2. B	2. D	2. three quarters
3. C	3. D	3. A	3. They ate an equal amount of pizza.	3. D
4. B	4. D	4. B	4. C	4. C
5. D	5. A	5. B	5. 4	5. A
6. A	6. C	6. D	6. two	6. B

Challenge Question

Week 1: 10. **Week 2:** 17. **Week 3:** 72. **Week 4:** 18. **Week 5:** 28. **Week 6:** 3. **Week 7:** Answers may vary. **Week 8:** 11. **Week 9:** 88. **Week 10:** 116. **Week 11:** 10 pencils. **Week 12:** 23 + 35 = 58 years old. **Week 13:** 10, 30. **Week 14:** 20. **Week 15:** the left. **Week 16:** the dog is 7 leaves long, the fox is 6 leaves long. **Week 17:** 1 and 3. **Week 18:** 3 red cars. **Week 19:** a rectangle. **Week 20:** two halves.

Assessment

1. C	11. A	21. A
2. B	12. 11	22. C
3. 7 books	13. C	23. B
4. C	14. A	24. D
5. A	15. C	25. B
6. D	16. D	26. C
7. D	17. B	27. D
8. B	18. 15 markers	28. A
9. D	19. 5 people	29. C
10. C	20. C	30. D

31. B	41. A	51. C
32. B	42. A	52. A
33. D	43. D	53. B
34. 34 + 25 = 59	44. a bus	54. D
35. C	45. B	55. A
36. D	46. C	56. B
37. A	47. 6 buttons	57. C
38. 38, 58	48. C	58. D
39. B	49. D	59. C
40. D	50. A	60. They both have equal amounts.

COMMON CORE TEST SERIES

The goal of these workbooks is to provide mock state tests so students can increase confidence and test scores during actual test day.

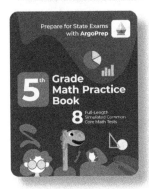

FrogYogi Math Series

It combines fun and engaging activities along with math concepts. Your child will be hooked in learning math on a daily basis. This workbook includes fun and effective yoga math breaks between solving problems helping the brain   relax and retain more information.

Award-Winning Program

500,000+ students, teachers and parents use ArgoPrep. Join the family!

**Mom's Choice
Gold Award**

**Homeschool Seal
of Approval**

**Parents's Choice
Gold Award**

**Education Hero
of The Year**

**National Parenting
Product Award**

**Tillywig Brain
Child Award**

**The EdTech Cool
Tool Award**

**The EdTech
Leadership Award**

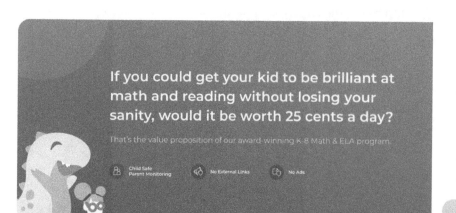

If you could get your kid to be brilliant at math and reading without losing your sanity, would it be worth 25 cents a day?

That's the value proposition of our award-winning K-8 Math & ELA program.

Child Safe
Parent Monitoring   No External Links   No Ads

Premium

FREE ~~9.99$~~
SAVE 100%

- 30,000+ Practice Questions
- 500+ Video Lectures
- 15,000+ Video Explanations
- Printable Worksheets
- 14 Days Free Trial
- One subscription for all your kids
- Progress Reporting

VISIT ARGOPREP.COM/K8

Take a look inside!

Your Child Moves Ahead of the Class With ArgoPrep

K-8 Math and ELA Video Lectures

Your subscription includes ALL grades so you can access video lessons from different grades. We cover and teach every topic your child needs to know for their grade level! All of our video lessons are taught by licensed-teachers and the videos are designed to be engaging!

Gap-Proofing Quizzes

Our quizzes gauge student mastery level of any particular topic. If your child struggles, each quiz question has an explanation video to accompany it, so students don't fall through those "learning gaps". If they need more information, they can always review last year's videos and worksheets as well.

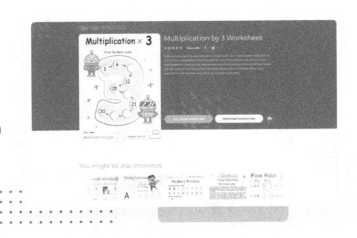

Unlimited Printable Worksheets

Print your worksheets from our database of thousands! We are constantly creating new, educator-approved worksheets for grades K-8 in our ever-expanding resource collection! Our worksheets are unique because we include fewer questions and more visually balanced spaces. Our amazing illustrations are 100% kid-approved!

KIDS WINTER ACADEMY

Kids Winter Academy by ArgoPrep covers material learned in September through December so your child can reinforce the concepts they should have learned in class. We recommend using this particular series during the winter break. This workbook includes two weeks of activities for math, reading, science, and social studies. Best of all, you can access detailed video explanations to all the questions on our website.

9 781951 048648